Oh God, our Maker, from this hour fourth we place ourselves in Thy Hands and submit ourselves to the discipline and teaching of Thy Christ, our God, Source of all Wisdom, all life, and all love.

Lead me that whatever I do asking Thy guidance hour by hour, whether I drink a glass of water, or in whatever I eat, or read, or think, or do, that I may thus be led, step by step, to perfect health of body, joy of spirit, and abundant life. To help fulfill the purpose of the Universe.

THE MINNESOTA CONFERENCE
UNITED CHURCH of CHRIST
122 W. Franklin Ave., #323
Phone: 612-871-0359
Minneapolis, MN 55404
Fax: 612-870-4885

Rev. William K. Kaseman
Minister for the Conference

Rev. Katherine Gibson
Christensen
Interim Minister for Eastern
Association

Rev. John F. Roschen
Interim Minister for Western
Association
309 N. Nokomis, P.O. Box 305
Alexandria, MN 56308
Phone:
  800-958-1970 (MN)
  612-760-1970 (all other states)
  612-763-6549 (Office)

Rev. Joanne E. Stoughton
Minister for Southern
Association
1102 S.W. Ninth Avenue
Faribault, MN 55021-6842
Phone:
  507-334-7282 (Secretary)
  507-334-0314 (Office)

July 28, 1995

Ms. Maryann Shores
222 - N. Whitford • # 613
Fergus Falls, MN 56537

Dear Maryann:

Your compendium of assorted pieces which you have created and collected through the years surely reveals the wide reaches of your thinking and the depths of your soul. Such a comprehensive compilation defies sitting down to read it from cover-to-cover as one sits down to read a book; a person must keep it close by, pick it up when in need of some inspiration, and open it to almost any page to receive new insight.

This is to admit I have not read it from cover-to-cover, but I will have it, as you suggest, *for "sublimation"* ["elevation," "raising," "lift," "upheaval," "improvement"] *and "fulfillment"* ["effectuation," "realization," "attainment"]. I am confident that, reading from it on occasion, will take me into the regions of the *sublime-and-fulfilled*.

I recall when I was going about doing a thing on the Shalom curriculum (it was 20 years ago already!), you were into that theme as well--and this present piece of yours has certainly built on the peace-love-justice-wholeness emphasis.

Keep on thinking those good thoughts, Maryann.

Cordially,

John F. Roschen, interim
Minister for Western Association

I give you a new commandment; that you Love one another...
— John 13:34

THIS I COMMAND YOU: LOVE EACH OTHER.
— John 15:17

Learn Inclusive Love.
FROM LONLINESS TO ONENESS

PURPOSE —

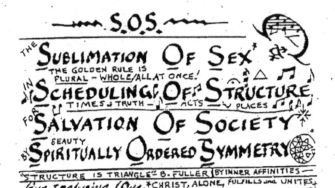

~~~ S.O.S. ~~~

THE **SUBLIMATION OF SEX** *
THE GOLDEN RULE IS PLURAL — WHOLE/ALL AT ONCE!

IN **SCHEDULING OF STRUCTURE**
TIMES & TRUTH — ACTS — PLACES

FOR **SALVATION OF SOCIETY**

BY BEAUTY **SPIRITUALLY ORDERED SYMMETRY**

STRUCTURE IS TRIANGLE" B. FULLER {BY INNER AFFINITIES}

Live Inclusive Love. * CHRIST, ALONE, FULFILLS and UNITES US BY WHAT IS DEEPEST IN US.

Inspiration for much of this material came from the works of Teilhard de Chardin.

SEE: <u>VERSES DISTILLED FROM TEILHARD</u> - *by Maryann Shorea*

222, North Whitford • # 613
Fergus Falls; Minnesota 56537

Note to my children!

I am still struggling to get my book out. The more I see of the "Evening News", and the statistics of the hunger, disease, and abuse of children; the more certain I am that a total change of human consciousness is vital. There needs to be a Light so paralyzing that all will change their focus for living. The only power (as I say in the book) strong enough and general enough to do this would be erotic Love transformed, controlled, scheduled, and arranged by a Holy Spirit. Inclusive Love is like our family - very diverse and various.

"From wrong to wrong the exasperated spirit proceeds, unless restored
by that refining fire where you must move in measure, like a dancer".
— T.S. Eliot

Love,
Mom — August 1993

This book is
dedicated to —
Lennis and Mary Mitchell
— who corrected and inspired my
research, for the necessary questioning
(and understanding) of
the "human condition".

5

Love is in process of "changing state." And it is in this new direction that the collective passing of humanity into One is being prepared. All this Love needs for its realization is that the appeal of the divine personal Centre be strongly enough felt to conquer the attraction of nature convergence at a higher level.

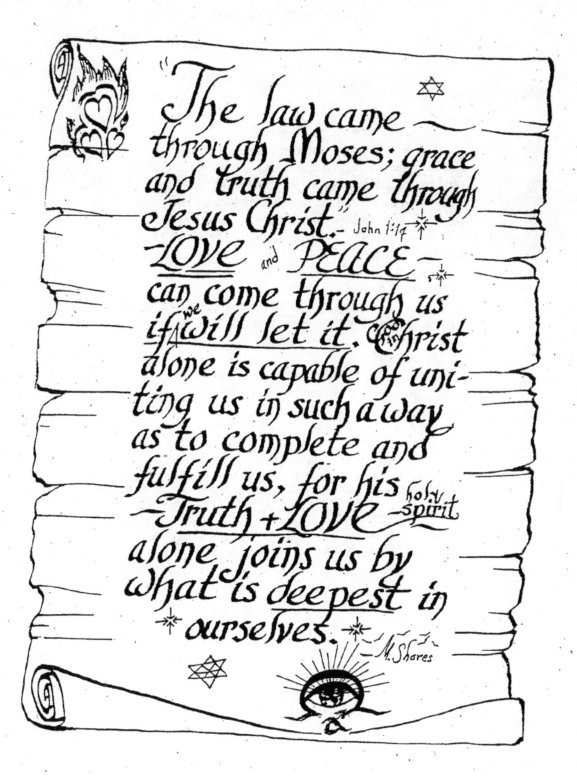

"The law came through Moses; grace and truth came through Jesus Christ." – John 1:17 LOVE and PEACE can come through us if we will let it. Christ alone is capable of uniting us in such a way as to complete and fulfill us, for his Truth + LOVE holy spirit alone joins us by what is deepest in ourselves. – M. Shores

Do not let what is good to you be spoken of as evil.

— ROMANS 14:16

When a society becomes very liberal there is usually a puritanical rebound which produces perversions and atrocities because of the repression. The first victims of the purges are those whose expressions of LOVE embarrass the loveless, who are quick to judge and condemn.

Love is the most powerful force in the world, drawing and holding all things together. It becomes short circuited in some way when it is not allowed to express. The variety of experiences are stages of a humanity growing up.

Inclusive, accepting LOVE is the change impelling, forward moving power of life, an incoming tide that cannot be turned back nor always effectively channeled within all our traditions and restrictions.

Our sins, which are many, are forgiven when we love much. ("Her sins which are many are forgiven for she loved much" - Jesus)

THAT IS THE DIFFERENCE BETWEEN THE EASTERN RELIGIONS AND CHRISTIAN RELIGION, BETWEEN BUDDHA AND TEILHARD: EASTERN MYSTICISM = REGRESSION INTO THE UNCREATED. CHRISTIAN MYSTICISM = INTEGRATION BY LOVE AND ATTACHMENTS IN GOD'S CREATION, (STILL IN PROGRESS) WE LIVE IN THE CHRISTIAN IDEAL OF INDIVIDUAL SALVATION (THE "OCEAN" HAS ITS COMPONENTS - NO TWO ALIKE) HOLY ARRANGEMENT IN INFINITE AND ETERNAL BEING IS OUR GOAL, IDENTITY INTEGRATED IN ONE.

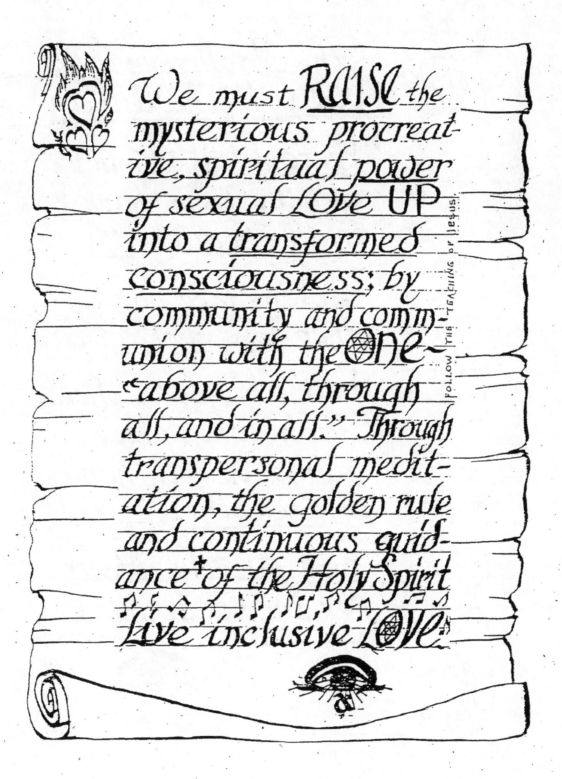

We must RAISE the mysterious procreative, spiritual power of sexual LOVE UP into a transformed consciousness; by community and communion with the ONE "above all, through all, and in all." Through transpersonal meditation, the golden rule and continuous guidance* of the Holy Spirit. Live inclusive LOVE.

FOLLOW THIS SPIRITUAL TEACHING OF JESUS.

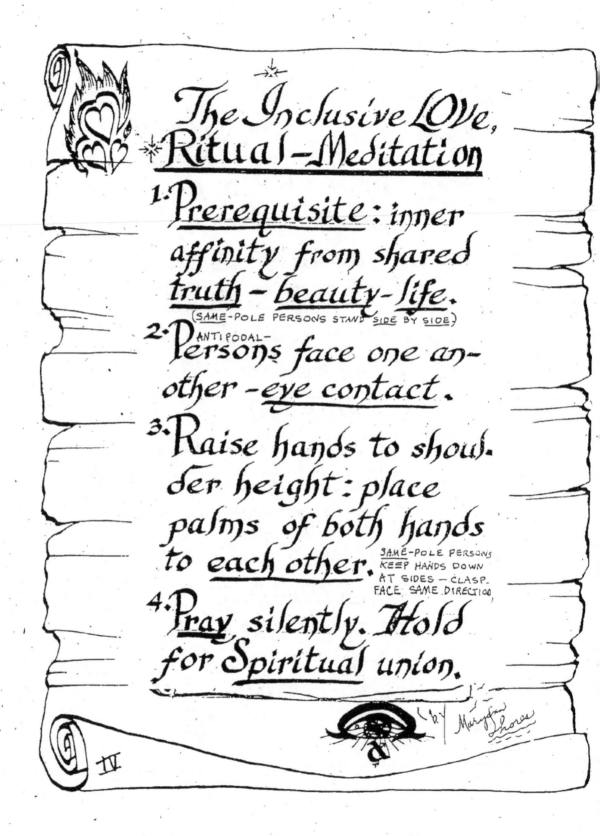

The Inclusive LOVE, Ritual–Meditation

1. **Prerequisite**: inner affinity from shared **truth – beauty – life**.
   (SAME-POLE PERSONS STAND SIDE BY SIDE)

2. ANTIPODAL – **Persons** face one another – **eye contact**.

3. **Raise** hands to shoulder height: place palms of both hands to **each other**. SAME-POLE PERSONS KEEP HANDS DOWN AT SIDES – CLASP FACE SAME DIRECTION

4. **Pray** silently. **Hold** for **Spiritual union**.

by Mary Ann Shores

IV

Transpersonal Prayer
The Inclusive Love meditation ritual.

(OPTIONAL, OF COURSE.)

The purpose of the
Inclusive LOVE medi-
tation ritual is to realize
the "numinous" element of
LOVE, the Holy Being –
"above, through, and in all."
To become aware of the
heights and depths of the
Tremendous Mystery, be-
yond the material world.
By familiarity with transcendance, fear of death is
dispelled, and Inclusive
LOVE is found, which includes
all commitments in an ordered, scheduled whole.

—LIVING-IN-LIFE; DYING-IN-LOVE. —H. Shores

♪ *a Purpose for Life* ♪

To *find* a socially acceptable, ecstatic and ful-
filling demonstration
of *LOVE*, for *each* significant other, in private
Spiritual ritual, and
affinity group meetings,
replacing, effectively,
the urge for biological
sexual expression, or
perversions, with a
higher, *triune* social
structure, *scheduled* and
arranged like music. ♪

V

Mary Ann Shores

The Organizing of Love-Structure

A SOLUTION to many of the social problems of these days, (extreme materialism and waste, drug abuse, alcoholism, loneliness, depression and despair) could be found in SCHEDULING TIME for Love, and truth.

For example: Besides arranging time for your children, (if you are divorced and remarried,) allow one or two hours a month to your former spouse! INCLUSIVE LOVE requires that when someone loves you, you must give that person a little of your TIME.

'What intolerable suffering, caused by separation, could be alleviated by SCHEDULING TIME for each person LOVE has drawn to you.' People would no longer feel that they are victims of circumstances.

> "Men should not be the creatures of circumstance;
> circumstances should be the creatures of men."-
> Thomas Carlisle

We can wait with patience for a CERTAIN good to come.

The future of human life on Earth depends upon an advance in human unity. The first step in that direction is to recognize the reality of specific inner affinities: That LOVE IS.

Until death, quality of life requires SCHEDULING of many activities. SCHEDULE time for many LOVES: Your parents, children, spouse, friends, soul-mates, and special small groups in community. The REGULARITY OF A SCHEDULED EXPRESSION OF INNER LIFE WILL BE THE FOUNDATION OF A NEW, FUNCTIONING, WHOLE EARTH.

Turn the suffering of separation into anticipation of an hour that will come! Something to look forward to and plan for.

The chaotic human race must begin to build an organic STRUCTURE at the BASE of society, for future harmony, beauty of order, and peace.

— Maryann Shores

MAKE COPIES TO DISTRIBUTE.

Structured Love
(Requires individual adaptation.)

New Social Structure →
SEE: ROMANS 14:16-19

JUST AN EXAMPLE OF A POSSIBLE –

Inclusive, Triune Love △ Schedule

☆ (PRE-SET TIMES IMPORTANT FOR PREPARATIONS.)
(ANTICIPATION.)

1. DAILY PRAYER/MEDITATION – ½ HR. EARLY ÷ GOD
SPIRITUAL GUIDANCE.

2. SPOUSE – 1 HR. PER WEEK – "QUALITY TIME."

3. EACH CHILD – ½ HR. PER WEEK

4. SOUL-MATE – 1 HR. PER MONTH { LIMITED TO MAINTAIN SPIRITUAL CONTENT. } OR FORMER SPOUSE.
IF UNGIVEN SUBSTITUTE ITEM 10...OR 6

5. COMMUNAL WORSHIP – 1 HR. PER WK.

6. TWELVE SIGNIFICANT FRIENDS – ½ HR. A PER MO (EACH)

7. SELF CULTIVATION – DEVELOPMENT – 1 HR. PER WK.
STUDY – NEW ABILITIES AND HOBBIES OR ALREADY ATTAINED SKILLS, ETC.

8. OPEN – FREE – UNSCHEDULED – 1 HR. PER WK.

9. DAILY WORK – 8 HRS. PER DAY ? { OTHER ⊕ NECESSITIES AS NEEDED. }

10. SMALL GROUP (AFFINITY) 1 HR. PER MO.

☆ See Book: TRIUNE LOVE

⊕ MOST TIME STILL REMAINS UNSCHEDULED.

– Maryann Shores

REAL _LOVE_ IS A PERSONAL, IDENTIFYING, ARRANGING AND CEMENTING, WHOLE-LIFE ACTIVITY, — OBEDIENT TO THE HOLY SPIRIT AND THE GOLDEN RULE, HOUR BY HOUR.

LOVE AND STRUCTURE

Love is the **drawing, identifying** and **arranging** spirit of the universe. It continuously creates more and higher consciousness. It is internal to creation, Permeating all that exists.

The purpose of love is structure, synthesis, integration, and the functioning of the universe in harmony and freedom. ("Freedom" is the ability to act from internal truth rather than from external coercion, law, or convention. "Truth" is the awareness and expression of things as they are.)

There are as many levels of love as there are points on a line, each with its own radius of energy. But the highest love is born from and sustained by shared truth—resulting in mutual understanding and interaction.

Love cannot be maintained if it is cut off from the one uniting Mind of the universe. It is always more or less perverted, abused, and distorted when it is controlled by individual will without reference to the good of all. There are four components of the best human love: the right persons, in the right places, at the right time, engaged in the right action and expression. This discriminating process includes children, pets, other adults, and the whole cosmos!

Love must include new complexities, with time, because it is a living, growing reality continuously building on accumulated past associations. If there is marriage, it is simply the second stage in a series of intense inclusive commitments based upon personal, internal affinities, by the spirit of the whole.

Love creates (and sustains) **identity** by relationship. It must be allotted certain times for its growth and development. As with music, time is part of its structure. Times of truth, and right timing of our loves, should be the primary activity of living. Because time does not pass but accumulates.

When we love we are as tendrils of the universe groping to become. Jesus was killed (and misunderstood) but He was the seed planted in the earth, crumbling the clods of ages, that love might grow. We are called to arrange ourselves and the world by means of faithful, successive, and inclusive love relationships. These associations provide motivation and power to build consciousness on the earth until all creatures are **aware** of **being** various parts of **one life.**

"Structure is triangle." — Buckminster Fuller
Creation - Complexity - Consciousness ➤ Christ
the purpose of Love is STRUCTURE,
for life and freedom.
Identity in eternal relationships of beauty and order.

SEE - John 3:17 & Ephesians 1:9-10

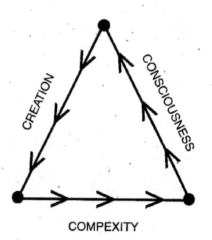

COMPEXITY

"God IS Love."

<u>CREATING</u> BY <u>UNITING PARTS.</u>

THE ACTION AND BREATH OF HIS HOLY SPIRIT, "BLOWING WHERE IT WILL."

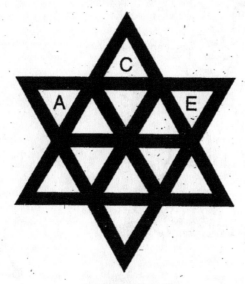

ACCELERATED
CHRISTIAN
<u>EVOLUTION:</u>
ACE

Love IS THE FREE AND IMAGINATIVE OUTPOURING OF THE <u>SPIRIT</u> OVER ALL UNEXPLORED PATHS.
—TEILHARD DE CHARDIN
(p.54, THE FUTURE OF MAN)

God is Love—

DRAW, COLOR AND POST

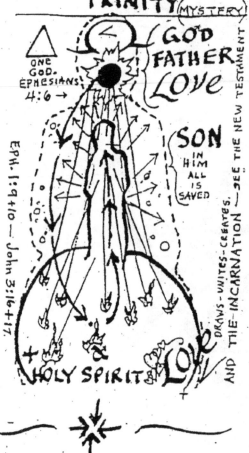

UNDERSTAND THE TRINITY (MYSTERY)

ONE GOD. EPHESIANS 4:6 →

GOD FATHER LOVE

SON IN HIM ALL IS SAVED

EPH. 1:9+10 — John 3:16+17.

DRAWS - UNITES - CREATES - SEE THE NEW TESTAMENT AND THE INCARNATION —

HOLY SPIRIT LOVE

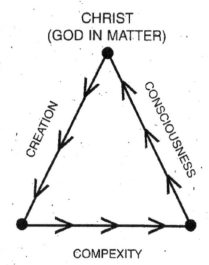

CHRIST
(GOD IN MATTER)

CREATION

CONSCIOUSNESS

COMPEXITY

For best beginning read the New Testament & (The Gospel of Thomas) —and all the works of Teilhard (de Chardin)

READ THE WORD "GOD" AS "LOVE", WHEREVER FOUND.
SEE - I John 4:16

18

LOOK UP THE REFERENCES

A Ballad of Truth

Faster and faster the changes come.
The Spirit within is creating!
  From
The troubles we suffer in human
  thought
A fresh tide of life! We are being
  brought
To see, anew, at a rapid pace,
As science opens time and space,
                         our second
  Breath:
"The Spirit of Truth" which has
  been sent
To Lead us into the All Truth
  Event.
We are one in excitement of knowing
  the real,
One in the Love we can both see and
  feel.
For the coming of the Wholly One
Is the Second Coming of the Son.
                    —Maryann Shores 1981

John 16:13   +EPH. 1:10

"Though I bestow all my goods
to feed the poor; and though
I give my body to be burned
and have not LOVE, it profits
me nothing." —1st CORINTHIANS 13:3

*POEM PUBLISHED IN THE INTERNATIONAL COMPENDIUM—
THE DESIRE TO BE HUMAN - EDITORS: ZONNEVELD AND MULLER

INFINITE - INCLUSIVE - *LOVE* — ALL SPACE/TIME — PRESENT —

DRAWS AND HOLDS ALL TOGETHER — IDENTITY IN COMPLEXITY — OMEGA

ONE IN ALL: ALL IN ONE. (INDIVIDUALS IDENTIFIED) IN ONE CONSCIOUSNESS COMPLEX

TOTAL CONSCIOUSNESS

WHOLE - SUM - NESS

HIGHER WHOLENESS

MEDITATION

REFLECTION

ORTHO - COGNITION

CREATIVITY

ASSIMILATION

STRUCTURE — INCLUSIVE UNITY — ETERNAL NOW — ONE

SOUL

③.

Jesus

✝

☩ ET. AL.

SYNTAXIC LEVEL

MINDFULNESS
COMMUNION
EGO - INTEGRATIONS
SUPER - CONSCIOUS
(FACETED STRUCTURE)
(SPIRITUAL MOTIVATION)
AND FREEDOM
NUMINOUS
CONTINUITY

NOOSPHERE

COMMUNION

ART   MUSIC, ET AL
MYTH
RITUAL
& INCLUSIVE, IDENTIFYING LOVE
DREAMS
(INDIVIDUALIZED)
ARCHETYPES
(IMAGES, ETC. — UNIVERSAL PRE-CONSCIOUS)

ORGANIZATION — ORDER — MOVING TOWARD

PARATAXIC LEVEL

EGO PRESENT — COMMUNICATES
PRECONSCIOUS + CONSCIOUS
SOUL - MATING PROBABLE
USE OF IMAGES and EMOTIONS

(LIST: ARTISTS, POETS,
INVENTORS, COMPOSERS
ETC. ETC.)

②.

BIOSPHERE

PRE-INTELLECTUAL

REFLEX - IONS
AUTOMATISMS (ALSO SEX - MOBS - ARMIES)
"TONGUES"
(AUTOMATIC WRITING - GLOSSOLALIA, ETC.)
PROACTIVE DRUGS
HYPNOTISM
(SURRENDER OF MIND) (CULTS)
(MEDIUMS) (SHAMANS, ETC.)
TRANCE
(DEMON POSSESSION, ETC.)
SCHIZOPHRENIA →
CHAOS
&
ALPHA

Spirit — Energy — LOVE — Moving Toward

①.

PROTAXIC

PROTOTAXIC LEVEL

ABANDONED SELF OR
LACK OF EGO   (NO CONSCIOUS, THOUGHTFUL CONTROL)
UNCONSCIOUS
PHYSICAL MATING PROBABLE
BODILY RESPONSES

("PSYCHIC" EXPRESSIONS ON LEVELS 1. + 3.)
ALL LEVELS SOMETIMES EMERGE - EFFERVESCE.

HUMAN CATEGORIES (OVERLAP)

BASED ON John C. Gowan and Teilhard de Chardin   by Maryann Shores

SEE THE GOSPEL OF JOHN
SEE FIRST CORINTHIANS, CHAPTERS 12, 13, & 14

What Love Does

When suffering comes
(As it will) to you
Enter it with all you do
Do not seek for an escape
Suffering is a human fate
On accepting it your life depends
Sometimes alone; sometimes with friends
In music, poetry and arts
You will meet with broken hearts
In nature and in silence too
The darkness then must comfort you
By candle-light and setting sun
Feel the pain that has begun
Suffering hid in every soul,
The mystery that makes one
                    Whole.

Eternal Love

I come to you an abject heap
I come to you in prayer (and sleep)
My wholly melted self so weak
My mind so fogged I cannot speak
My strength poured out upon the ground
My mouth too dry to make a sound
My days and years too short-too long.
My Love, my life, a wailing song
Oh help me for I need to see
There is Eternal Love* in Thee.

"The process is so marked that anyone
who takes the trouble to analyse the
economic-technical-social forces...
spreading over the whole world,...
will find it impossible to escape
the force that draws us together...
It would be completely useless
to try to build up anything that
could stand against our eventual
unity."   -Teilhard de Chardin

—*wholesome-wholeness—

The Tree of Consciousness.

(THE EVOLUTION OF CONSCIOUSNESS)

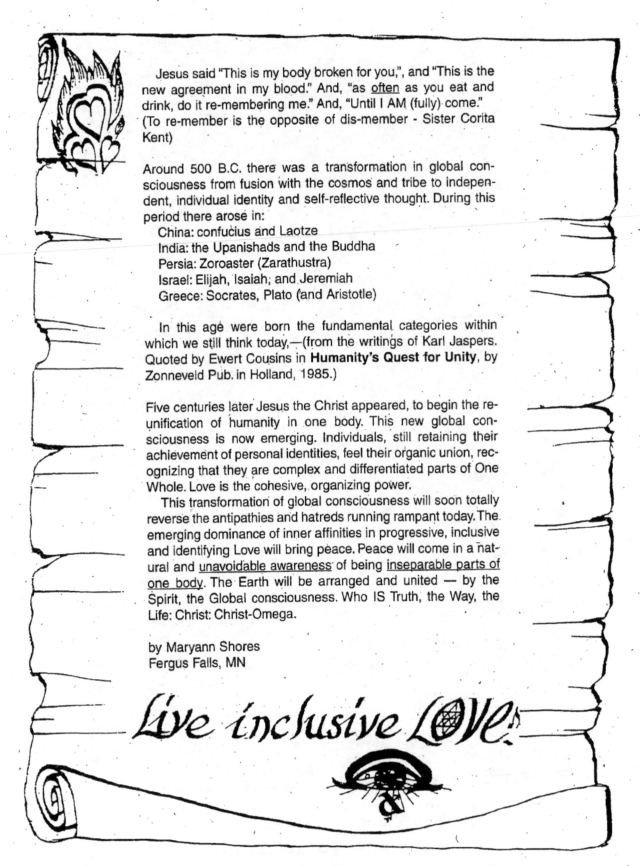

Jesus said "This is my body broken for you,", and "This is the new agreement in my blood." And, "as <u>often</u> as you eat and drink, do it re-membering me." And, "Until I AM (fully) come." (To re-member is the opposite of dis-member - Sister Corita Kent)

Around 500 B.C. there was a transformation in global consciousness from fusion with the cosmos and tribe to independent, individual identity and self-reflective thought. During this period there arose in:

China: confucius and Laotze
India: the Upanishads and the Buddha
Persia: Zoroaster (Zarathustra)
Israel: Elijah, Isaiah, and Jeremiah
Greece: Socrates, Plato (and Aristotle)

In this age were born the fundamental categories within which we still think today,—(from the writings of Karl Jaspers. Quoted by Ewert Cousins in **Humanity's Quest for Unity**, by Zonneveld Pub. in Holland, 1985.)

Five centuries later Jesus the Christ appeared, to begin the re-unification of humanity in one body. This new global consciousness is now emerging. Individuals, still retaining their achievement of personal identities, feel their organic union, recognizing that they are complex and differentiated parts of One Whole. Love is the cohesive, organizing power.

This transformation of global consciousness will soon totally reverse the antipathies and hatreds running rampant today. The emerging dominance of inner affinities in progressive, inclusive and identifying Love will bring peace. Peace will come in a natural and <u>unavoidable awareness</u> of being <u>inseparable parts of one body</u>. The Earth will be arranged and united — by the Spirit, the Global consciousness. Who IS Truth, the Way, the Life: Christ: Christ-Omega.

by Maryann Shores
Fergus Falls, MN

Live inclusive LOVE

THE EMERGING SPIRITUAL/SOCIAL PARADIGM

Recent (and historical) sexual scandals should produce the realization that something is seriously wrong with our conventions and traditions, and reveal a new vision of Love.

TRACE CONSCOUSNESS IN A BIOLOGY TEXT

It is the simplistic attitude of "either/or" that is to blame for separating and disintegrating individuals and groups in unstructured chaos. Intense, spontaneous Love needs freedom but must be inclusive, and structured in both time and space. When will people recognize that the human personality is a faceted structure requiring many fitting faces for fulfillment? The need is for variety and appropriate expression of each facet of Love: a different mode of being in relationship to each person which would fully express the uniqueness of each, person, time and situation. Then each of these associations could have the impact, power, and uniting force experience in sexual expression at its best. We need new translations of Love: new ways of giving to and receiving, wholly, another person.

As returning completely to a simpler life style is not only impossible but regressive, so returning to polygamy as it was practiced in ancient times and in primitive societies would be disintegration of civilization. But a new social structure built on spiritual affinities, and flexible as music is the "wave of the future". Marriages and other ties must be component parts not eliminated! (Libertarians do not recognize the primacy of the Spirit and inner affinity.)

There should be scheduling and structure of real Love in human occurrences. One who does not respond to another when there is a strong inner affinity is less than his best self. As human beings we are required to Love.

If a relationship becomes primarily physical it deteriorates. If it has no tangible, physical expression it evaporates. Pain in Love is evidence of its importance. The problem is one of rightness of fulfillment of each soul when "deep calls unto deep".

CREATIVE RITUALS violating no one's person or higher self elevates life for the individual and society as a whole. Creative self-giving requires self-denial and self-sacrifice but produces beauty and strength of character. Cold, severe, and rigid repression and self-righteousness result in judgmental, vindictive personalities and societies. On the other hand, easy, shallow, sub-human sexual exploits disintegrate the individual and society. Commitment, identification of persons, and the honoring of inner affinity brings elevation of society and continued evolution of humanity (and the individual).

A SYSTEM OF SUBLIMATION EQUAL TO THE POWER OF BIOLOGICAL SEX; THE TIMING, SCHEDULING, INTEGRATION AND ARRANGEMENT OF MANY LOVES.

Therefore close relationships are to be inclusive, identifying and progressing like the harmonies of music. Or the changing designs in a kaleidoscope in which the pieces of colored glass change position in space and time but are always included in the new configuration.

Everything we do or think is tinged by our sexual identity. As I have said in another place it is SUBSTITUTION of one person by another, or by other things such as money, drugs, or work, which is adultery. The Golden Rule is the perfect law of Love: Do unto others just what you would want them to do to you. This eliminates all kinds of evil such as rape, abuse, and domination, and requires a sensitivity to another's needs and desires. (Notice that the Golden Rule is

"IN THE <u>NAME</u> OF JESUS (OR CHRIST)"
MEANS, "IN THE NATURE OF..."
AND SHOULD BE READ THAT WAY.

READ DAILY — PEOPLE CANNOT LIVE ON FOOD ALONE. READ AT RANDOM IN THE NEW TESTAMENT DAILY. MARK VERSES FOR FUTURE USE. MINE THE TRUTH AND INTEGRATE IT INTO LIFE! — M. Shores

the LORD'S PRAYER
IN THE PRESENT TENSE
"TREMENDOUS MYSTERY"
HOLY BEING, One
Spirit, Light. Our Father
(Above all — through all and in all)...
Holy is your name.
Love is Love
Your ORDER comes; your will is Being done in the Earth as it is in the whole Universe.
You give us, this day, our daily food, and fulfill our needs, as we fulfill the needs of others. Forgiving our debts as we forgive.
You do not lead us into temptation, but deliver us from all evil. FOR YOURS IS...
THE ....
RULE OF TRUTH
the Power of LOVE
and the
Glory of Life
..... FOREVER. †

— COLOR — CUT OUT — USE — AS BIBLE BOOK-MARK

THE FOLLOWSHIP OF JESUS THE CHRIST.

I pledge allegiance to the Earth.
One planet indivisible.
And to the Universe in which she lives:
One system, under God.
With freedom and fulfillment
For the highest life
and Consciousness of all.

COPY ➤
USE
ON
LETTERS
AND
PACKAGES

plural.) Every moment requires the weighing of Love against other demands by the application of the Golden Rule in its important plural form.

The observable goal of life ever since it began on Earth is continually more and higher consciousness. This can only be consummated by progressively uniting all things in greater and greater functioning complexity, by the power called Love which draws and holds it all together.

TRIUNE SOCIAL STRUCTURE AND PEACE

As we witness the accellerating break up of nations and the disintegration of cities and marriages why doesn't it occur to anyone that God may be trying to tell us something? When an old paradigm is being replaced there must be a period of chaos before the new truth takes over. My thesis is that human society is evolving as a whole, leaving behind the physical structuring based on dyadic relationships. As Buckminster Fuller pointed out, "Structure is triangle." We see this in all the higher human occupations: architecture, music, literature, and political negotiations.

The "Eternal Triangle" is the base for movement toward the complexity necessary for a new consciousness. (It is interesting to note that Abraham had two wives; Jacob married first Leah and then Rachel; and as stated in the New Testament, Jesus Loved Martha, Mary, Lazarus, and John. It is also no accident that God, who is Love, is triune, a trinity.

Love someone . . . . (else, too.)

One Love, ✡ many faces.

The world struggling for some kind of functioning unity must come to understand that there is no stability of structure until there is triunity. The triad is basic to all natural configurations.

Conventional marriage is a good example of what happens to dyadic "structure". With the passing of time, the partners must either include others, individually, or the petrified union crumbles to dust in one way or another. In the mutual idolatry of a conventional marriage if the partners try to prevent the extension and growth of Love, the result is the spiritual death of one or both persons.

On the other hand, casual and promiscuous relationships disintegrate human beings because they are based on physical attraction alone and are regressive to the Animal Kingdom's pattern of mating. People involved in this kind of life-style deteriorate from lack of Center, depth and fulfillment of Love.

Where there is faith and communion with God in truth, beauty, and awe there is Love. But some old religious practices and beliefs no longer mediate the Spirit and are like the "old garment" from which the "new patches" simply tear away. The astonishing prevalence of "sexual misconduct" by many religious leaders is the result of their openness to the Holy Spirit! It is, in some cases, because of their sensitivity to the drawing power of Love, not some activity of Satan! They simply do not understand what is happening and choose the wrong solutions to the problems that arise.

Triune Love is structured by inner affinities. The satisfaction of these Spiritual hungers are as

29

necessary to truly human life and the growth of higher consciousness as food and drink are necessary to the body.

Persons conscientiously living out the triadic social structure based on inner affinity are open to Life and growth because it is the natural arrangement for human development, not a comfortable dead end. It contains Power.

As with Buckminster Fuller's geodesic domes and spheres, the "tensegrity" necessary is the triangle. A triangle keeps the corners apart to prevent collapse of the structure. This is just as true of the human triangles important to the structure of stable societies. The attention required to live well in this triune culture diminishes human interest in political power struggles, the escapism of drugs, and the predominance of acquiring things. That is why triunity is essential to the new world order which will bring peace to the world. It will lift the common people to uncommon heights. In harnessing the usually uncontrolled powers of sex and Love, the human race will orbit at a higher level around the One Center of Life.

Life results from the action of Love which is the power that draws and holds all things together. As Teilhard de Chardin teaches in his many books, individual parts are drawn togther creating first matter, then by the resulting complexity: life. Greater complexity produces consciousness, and in this way complexity-consciousness completes the creation of the Earth.

Jesus taught his disciples that divorce causes adultery. He also taught that to be lured by passing physical attractions is adultery. (Adultery is the substitution of a person by another person, thing, or activity.) It is time to learn INCLUSIVE LOVE, scheduled in time, arranged in space, and controlled so that Jesus' only command, that we should Love each other, and obey the Golden Rule: "Do unto others just what you would want them to do to you" may bring individual and social vitality and peace. We need to research human relationships to sustain living and Loving on Earth

The scheduling and arranging of Love in time and space is just as necessary to the structure of human life as it is in music. In the inevitable changing of relationships, progression is essential from every dissonant chord to an harmonic resolution.

Time does not pass but accumulates. "Past" relationships are imbedded in the subconscious (we are made of our relationships) and must be respected and maintained in their integrity. All the lacks in human life are being overcome: God overrules. "What man did not think could happen is the very thing God had prepared for those who Love him." Love, God present, takes precedence over law, God's past. The "Eternal Now" contains past, present and future in one dynamic whole beyond our capacity to comprehend. The drawing power of the living God continues to work in us: first, the individual person becomes integrated; second, two become one; third there is the triangle; and then an unending fibbonic progression (1+2+3+5+8+13,et: (Jesus and his original disciples illustrate the structure of thirteen persons.)

There must be a universal structure for Love beyond the family unit and casual friendships. The soul is offered its mates for depth of Love and new growth. In this we experience the reality and power of God. Maturity and the cultivation of the inner life is required, just as maturity of body is required for physical mating. The "Eternal Triangle" is the basic unit necessary for the continued development of humanity. The jealousies and possession complexes of the past are obsolete. After the triad has matured, persons find that they are Spiritually called to all those in similar streams of consciousness and wholeness of outlook.

Love is born of sharing truth, beauty, and all motivation toward wholeness of all life. Those who desire Love must know that their desire is for God, the "One above, through and in all."

More and greater Love is the essential bonding necessary for the structure of peace: A new consciousness of the Earth, shared by all, INCLUSIVE, organized Love, the living, growing basic reality of human life and hope for the future.

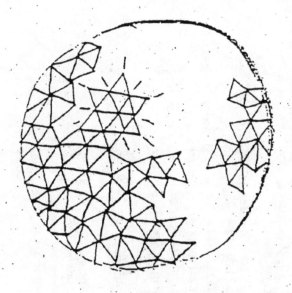

GEODESIC
SOCIAL STRUCTURE
GROWING IN THE
EARTH.

*...the Kingdom
of the Father is
spread upon the
earth and men
do not see it.*
-Jesus (the Gospel according to Thomas)

Whatever has been, is.
We <u>know</u> that by Love we are
already (and forever) one.

The Omega Cone of LOVE

- Read from bottom to top.

Total complexity

-Consciousness (each identity defined by relationship) co-extensive with the whole.
see - 1st Corinth. 13:12

Triune
△ - Tensegrity 1 John 4:16 faithful - inclusiveness: Inclusive, identifying love.
Col. 1:20
Eph. 4:10

Luke 4:18+19 - Jesus' Manifesto
John 3:16+17 - God's Purpose

-Communion - semi-voluntary choices
Most relationships determined by external causes: convenience, biology, conventions, tradition, etc.

Everything is good; nothing is perfect.

Life
Notice reciprocal development.
Increasing complexity: LIFE.
Group consciousness.
Involuntary associations - freedom limited by necessity.

Love draws, creates, includes, identifies, intensifies, unites......

One above all, through all, and in all. ~Eph. 4:6

See quantum physics
random particles
little freedom given -
weak love/cohesion.

The Purpose of love is structure for life and freedom.

The right persons to the right persons at the right time.
Luke 15:21-
Logos Love

Voluntary Associations
Free and voluntary - union......
Faithful, Inclusive - Faceted Freedom
the Holy Spirit. Love - Strong cohesion -
Greater synergy
read "name" as "nature" in all of the Gospel of John.
Eph. 1:10

See: Science and Christ and other books by Teilhard de Chardin

Eternal (all time sustained)
The infinite
Eternal Life in Love.
Romantic Love
Triune Love
REALIZED INCARNATION
spiritual affinities
SPIRITUAL + COMMUNITY
MARRIAGE
3.
2.
NATURAL RELATIONSHIPS
1.
CONSCIOUS
$E=MC^2$

SOULS ----
With degrees of instant communion -
Old Testament level

Evil is lack of association: division, separation, maceration, disintegration, wrong re-uniting.
For right

Matter ----
More cohesion/love: creation of matter.

Continuously increasing consciousness!

Note: Each level includes all previous levels

—LOVE— energy ---- M & A
Father/Inseminator.
In the beginning God... the Word is Love......

DISCUSSION OF TWO DIAGRAMS
(L. James Koch = Q)

Q. Now, we are talking about the evolutuion of marriage and family life.

A. We are talking about the evolution of Love, itself, really. And the evolution of the Earth whose cause is Love.

Q. Therefore we are beginning with . . . .

A. Primary particles. (At the bottom of the diagram) The Alpha.

Q. Okay. To explain how Love begins, and changes, and matures. Right?

A. Right.

Q. We are diagrammatically explaining this process?

A. Yes, and not only how Love progresses and matures, but how Love accomplishes the maturity of the Earth.
At the bottom of the diagram there is the beginning: a very remote Love activity. (This comes in general, with modificaitons, from the thought of Teilhard de Chardin) At this level there is a very feeble cohesion among the particles. That is, the strength of Love is not felt strongly by the rudimentary particles that are being acted upon.

Q. What are these particles?

A. They are the primary stuff of creation. This is before life. This is prelife atomic and molecular attractions of cosmic energy/matter. That is the very beginning. Then as you go up the diagram, you have the involuntary specialization of matter (by this Power called Love.)

Q. Then something happens!?

A. A specialization of matter occurs. But as we go on we see that there are two processes going on at once, and this continues throughout time with the ascendancy always going to Love, which is the positive principle. At the left on the diagram you see the arrows pointing upward, indicating the direction of the Love process. On the right, you see the downward movement of entropy and disintegration, the falling away of those things not held by Love. We see order rising out of chaos accompanied by a sort of spray of disintegration following in its wake.
Inanimate matter is drawn together in different patterns, and as it is drawn together the compounds become more complex. Through this process of Love working on matter, life appears. As we move upward we see that the lower forms of life assimilate sensations, and at the next stage of development is consciousness. The higher levels of animal life are conscious, i.e. aware of being and non-being. Above that, we see on the diagram, that consciousness develops to the point of reflection and assimilation of concepts. (All this by Power not its own)
Going on up the diagram, the mind matures. Then there comes a crisis which involves personal identity, Love, and God. This process results in human freedom, or if the wrong choice or

33

a refusal to make a choice occurs, there is reversal or regression. But even this cannot, of course, be final.

Then we come up to the next level. At the left here, marriage is common. Semi-voluntary specialization of community appears at this point. I call this level semi-voluntary because, at this level people accept their social environment with only a few modificaitons, while later a more completely voluntary association of persons comes about. The modifications of social environment that occur at this level are the choosing of a few special friends, marriage partner, and membership in certain, probably pre-established groups. This is the era we are now in the process of modifying.

The present social crisis is caused by the evolution of human social structures into more complex, more intensely conscious groups of more complex and more aware individual persons, brought about by the swift spread of a common culture and universal communication capabilities.

So at the next level we find voluntary specialization of associations. The most important concept to be accepted at this point is the reality of the incarnation. We must be able to see God in other persons. Here we may have the phenomenon of soul-mating growing out of internal affinities and spiritual interpersonal communion. This is the concept which allows growth in the social structure in relation to human marriage.

Q. Can marriage as we know it today, evolve to a higher form of human intercourse?

A. The answer to that is that it is not marriage, itself, that will be evolving but the social structure that contians marriage. Marriage is a natural, rather fixed social institution. And marriage itself will remain pretty much as it is for some time, but will have to allow for the other and higher relationships.

At the very top, here, we get up into the clouds where things are not so specific.

Q. So what then is the apex of this concept of the evolution of eternal Love?

A. Eternal Love, requires eternal relationships which are the source of identity. So we become altogether One in God/Omega through Christ, "the unifying principle of the universe". There is, here, a simplified form of this diagram which I call the Christmas Tree. I think by studying that now, the whole evolution of Love in the universe can be better understood. I would also like to recommend Science and Christ, Human Energy, and Building the Earth by Teilhard de Chardin, who is the source of some of the above basic viewpoints.

THE VOCATION OF RELATIONSHIP

Think of the world as consisting of particles drawn together to create matter: above and including matter, a filigree of interdependent living things. Life is caught up in natural relationships. Beyond the natural relationships, represented on the human level by tribe, marriage, family and community, there are spiritual affinities which depend upon the continuing cohesion of the lower levels.

34

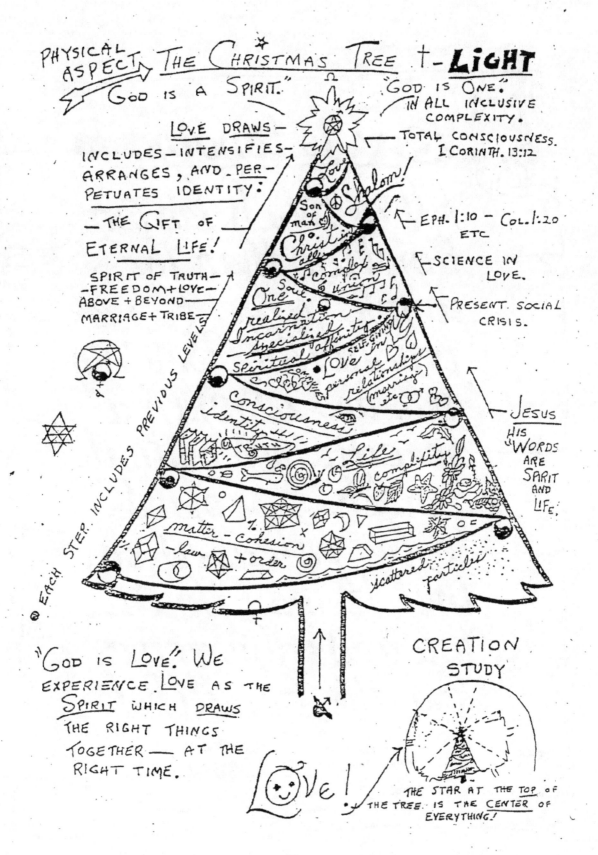

PHYSICAL ASPECT → THE CHRISTMAS TREE † - **LIGHT**

"GOD IS A SPIRIT."   "GOD IS ONE." IN ALL INCLUSIVE COMPLEXITY.

TOTAL CONSCIOUSNESS. I CORINTH. 13:12

LOVE DRAWS — INCLUDES — INTENSIFIES — ARRANGES, AND PERPETUATES IDENTITY.

— THE GIFT OF ETERNAL LIFE!

SPIRIT OF TRUTH — — FREEDOM + LOVE — ABOVE + BEYOND — MARRIAGE + TRIBE

EPH. 1:10 — COL. 1:20 ETC

SCIENCE IN LOVE.

PRESENT. SOCIAL CRISIS.

JESUS HIS WORDS ARE SPIRIT AND LIFE.

⊕ EACH STEP. INCLUDES PREVIOUS LEVELS

"GOD IS LOVE." WE EXPERIENCE LOVE AS THE SPIRIT WHICH DRAWS THE RIGHT THINGS TOGETHER — AT THE RIGHT TIME.

LOVE!

CREATION STUDY

THE STAR AT THE TOP OF THE TREE. IS THE CENTER OF EVERYTHING!

(within the tree:) Love • Shalom! • Son of man • Christ — all • complet. • union • One • Soul. • realized • Incarnation • Specialized • spiritual affinity • SELF-GIVING • Love in personal relationship (marriage) etc • consciousness • identity • Life • complexity • matter — cohesion — law + order • scattered particles

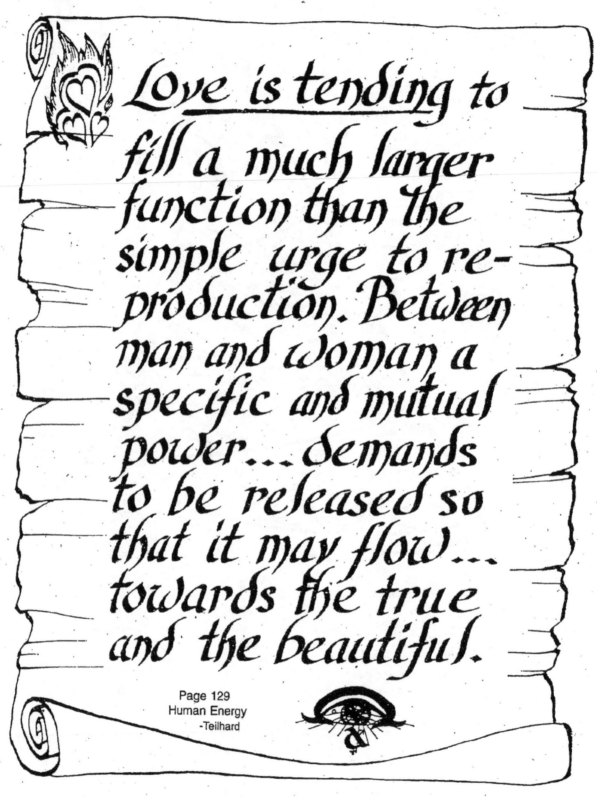

Love is tending to fill a much larger function than the simple urge to reproduction. Between man and woman a specific and mutual power.... demands to be released so that it may flow.... towards the true and the beautiful.

Page 129
Human Energy
-Teilhard

36

Marriage in relation to personal growth.

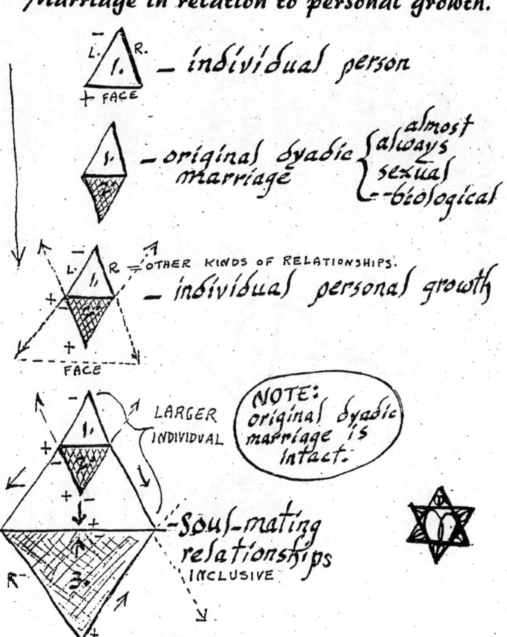

— individual person

— original dyadic marriage { almost always sexual — biological

OTHER KINDS OF RELATIONSHIPS.

— individual personal growth

LARGER INDIVIDUAL

NOTE: original dyadic marriage is intact.

— soul-mating relationships INCLUSIVE

Spiritual affinity increases with age and well-defined personal adentity.

37

Proclaiming the New COMMANDMENT (John 13:34) of Love.

FREE-HAND SKETCH OF
NEW LOGO FOR THE U.C.C.

by —
Maryann Shore

FERGUS FALLS, MN
56537

We must learn
inclusive love:

The Golden Rule is Plural.

REASONS
FOR
CHANGES

1. INSTEAD OF THE PRESENT LOGO CAPTION "That [we] may all be one", WE CONFESS THAT WE KNOW THAT WE ARE, ALREADY, "ALL ONE." ✝

2. THE OMEGA REPLACES THE CROWN BECAUSE IT DOES NOT MEAN OPPRESSION TO ANYONE, (AS THE CROWN SOMETIMES DOES.)

3. THIS CROSS REMINDS US, ALL WHO REALLY LOVE WILL SUFFER.

REAL LOVE REQUIRES STRUCTURE, AND GUIDANCE BY THE HOLY SPIRIT, FOR FULFILLMENT, AND FAITHFULNESS, AND.

RATIONALE

Love FLOWS FROM THE CROSS, ENGULFING THE

WHOLE
WORLD,

(AND BEYOND)

Christ AROSE TO FILL ALL THINGS." — EPH. 4:10
LOVE IS CHRIST'S COMMAND. —John 15:17

♀ — THE ALPHA SYMBOLIZES GOD'S SEED SOWN IN THE EARTH.

♂ — THE MALE SYMBOL IDENTIFIES JESUS.

FEMALE SYMBOL HONORS MOTHER EARTH.

Ω THE OMEGA ACKNOWLEDGES TRANSCENDANCE.

ALL ARE NOW ONE.

— *Maryann Shore* October 1995

38

God is Light diffused
—through all;
Christ, this Light defined...

The Spirit is this Light
in us...

Expressing through the
mind.

LOGO
RATIONALE:
(BOTTOM TO TOP)

1. FEMALE SYMBOL HONORS OUR MOTHER EARTH.

2. LAUREL - SYMBOL FOR PEACE FOR THE WHOLE WORLD, AND NATURE.

3. THE ALPHA, WITH MALE SYMBOL, REFERS TO CHRIST "PLANT-ED IN THE EARTH."

4. FISH:- CHRIST-IAN DISCI-PLINE.

5. WE ARE → ALREADY "ALL ONE."

6. THE EMPTY CROSS TEST-IFIES TO ETERNAL LIFE.

7. THE EYE OF GOD SYMBOL-IZES THE MIND AND NATURE OF GOD: PERSON-AL LOVE AND PRESENCE.

8. THE OMEGA SYMBOLIZES THE FULFILL-MENT OF ALL CREATION, IN CHRIST, BY THE HOLY SPIRIT.

MAKE A BANNER

OR THIS →

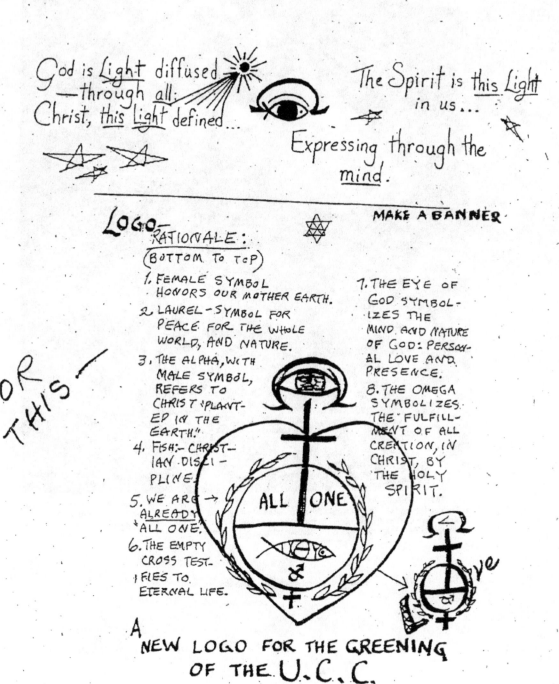

ALL ONE

Love

A NEW LOGO FOR THE GREENING OF THE U.C.C.

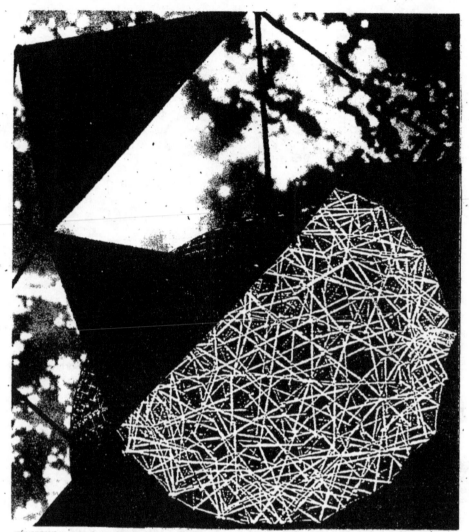

"TENSEGRITY" SPHERE — Inventor P. Buckminster Fuller invented a "Tensegrity" sphere which he describes as a bundle of rods and cables that can be made into a giant sphere so light and strong it can support a floating space station a mile in diameter. The rods don't touch each other, but are held in place by tension on the cables. The integrity of the sphere is such that repairs of any section do not disturb the rest of the geodesic integrity of the structure (AP Photo)

It is important to keep the "corners" apart!

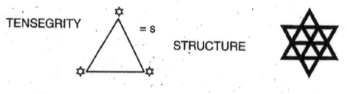

TENSEGRITY △ = S STRUCTURE

("One at my left and one at my right.")
- Jesus

HOLY ONE, HELP US TO LOVE PERFECTLY. — DOING OUR WORK IN THE WORLD WHILE WE ALSO DEVELOP AND MAINTAIN OUR SPIRITUAL AFFINITIES FOR THE <u>STRUCTURE</u> OF ABUNDANT AND ETERNAL LIFE.   AMEN.

THE ETERNAL TRIANGLE REVISITED

Fragments that are seeking one another, and not fragments that are parting, a world that is striving for unity, not a world that is disintegrating. A crisis of birth, and not symptoms of death. Essential affinities . . That is what we are witnessing . . (pp. 142).

When passion is most lofty and noble, the man and woman who come together meet only at the term of their spiritual growth. This law of human union is the law of our cosmic union. Christ holds us by the most material fibres of nature. Nevertheless we shall possess him perfectly only when our personal being, and the whole world with it have . . . reached the full limit of their unification. (pp, 76)

The unification that is being developed so intensely in our time in the human spirit and the human collectivity is the authentic continuation of the biological process that produced the human brain. That is what creative union means. (pp. 82) — SCIENCE AND CHRIST

Teilhard de Chardin

We have come to a time in the evolution of humanity when the involuntary and semi-voluntary relationships (determined by external causes events, convenience, and convention) are being complemented by more voluntary associations, which are the result of internal affinities, personal development, and spiritual needs.

In order to achieve freedom, fulfillment, greater being and a higher culture, mutual dependence builds a pattern of complex beauty, inclusive of all: the order created by passionate, personal Love, in an intricately structured social design, kept from disintegration by the "One above all, through all, and in all." It took us centuries to learn that Love is Trinity, Triad, Triune.

THE PURPOSE OF LOVE IS STRUCTURE FOR LIFE AND FREEDOM, IDENTITY IN ETERNAL RELATIONSHIPS OF BEAUTY AND ORDER. CREATION < COMPLEXITY < CONSCIOUSNESS < CHRIST.

We find the highest, holiest, deepest, and most fulfilling experience of Love in the Body of Christ, (the real and universal church). As a lover cherishes the parts of the body of the beloved, so we cherish the members of the Body. But we are joined in <u>order</u>. The neck-bone is not connected to the thigh-bone! (Although it cares about it)

The realization (and recognition) comes, that we are already One in Spirit, when we look into someone's eyes with whom we share this mystery. There are degrees of instant union/communion. Our mutual goal is to be totally one, functioning together in Love, and Truth.

Soul-Mating

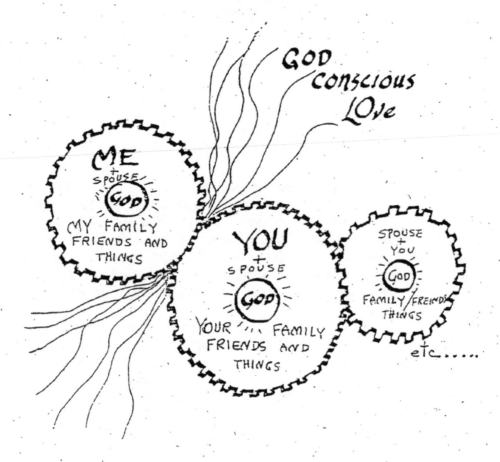

Spiritual Love does not supercede the natural; it is faithful to each and inclusive of all.

or

Imagine a many sided crystal-(the human soul). When LOVE, which is the Light and Power of God, draws two souls together they are bonded face to face. Others may bond to other facets, or come and go. Marriage is a physical bonding, but may <u>become</u> opaque. The LIGHT always permeates a LOVE kept Spiritual.

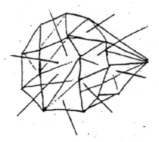

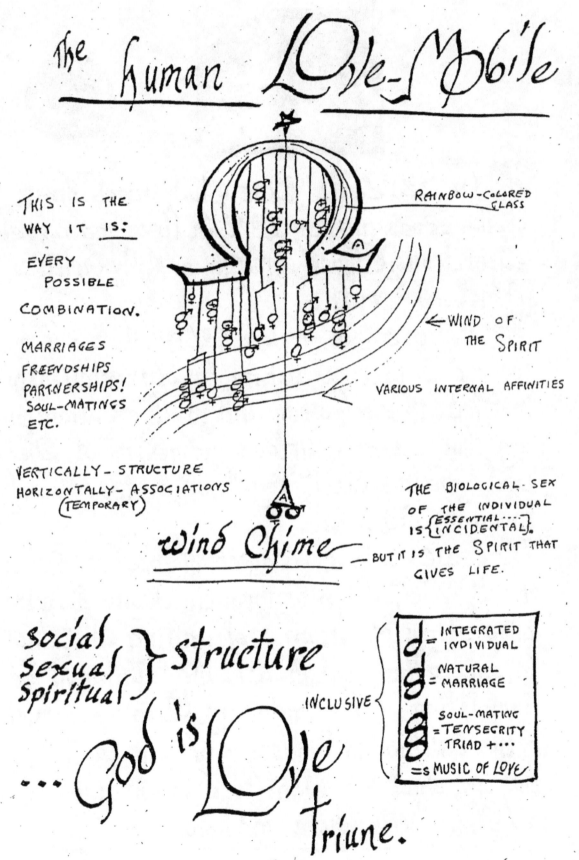

WRITE
A
STATEMENT
OF WHAT YOU
BELIEVE

We believe in One God, our Father,
Self-expressing by Love, in life, and revealed in Jesus Christ, through the Holy Spirit;
Word and Truth.
We believe that in Jesus, Christ, we live
forever identified in him by our relationships;
to God, to each other, and to all creation; knowing that we are various members of One
body, being built together by the One above,
through, and in all.
We believe in the power of the Holy Spirit,
the Love God gives through Jesus Christ
who alone is capable of uniting all things
in one Mind and Heart, the fulfillment and
completion of the maturing Universe, which
is the calling and mystery of our faith.
So we shall be identified in eternal life
in Love, forever here and now.
—M. Shores

44

INTERVIEW - with L. James Koch

Q. How basic is the marriage institution as it exists in current culture?

A. Well, one of the things that I would change about that question is, "as it exists". Marriage does not exist as it was intended, in most cases. I think that marriage is absolutely basic, something that cannot be surpassed until it is fulfilled. Very few can have more than marriage until they have had marriage! I like to use this analogy: it is something like Jesus said about the Law. That he did not come to abolish the Law but to fulfill it. Spiritual affinities must not replace marriage, but fulfill it.

Q. This leads then to the second question, in view of your whole thesis: Is the institution of dyadic marriage (that is the marriage of two persons), is that changing to a triadic or triune type of marriage? In which three beings are involved?

A. No. Not in the way that you have put it. This is where bigamy, polygamy, polyandry, commune marriages, mate-swapping, and all that kind of thing go wrong. Basic marriage is, and will continue to be, fundamental.

Q. Basic what marriage?

A. The original dyadic marriage is still the fundamental, basic relational structure. This is a very important point.

Q. Then what are you saying about the three persons?

A. Well, that is the basis of this book and the rest of the book explains this point. There has to be a triune structure for Love, first in marriage and later in soul-mating. But the original marriage must be maintained. What happens in divorce and remarriage, for instance, (and this is the reason that Jesus said that divorce is adultery) is that instead of going onward and upward there is regression. And instead of the basic two there is just a replacement there, at that level. And if you are going to talk about what adultery is, it is substitution.

Q. You use the words "eternal Love and tensegrity". (as the force causing individual integration natural marriage, and triadic structure.) What is tensegrity?

A. Tensegrity is the tension and integrity necessary to hold the whole thing together, by holding the components apart!

Q. Alright, lets get to the basic question then. What is the third party or the third person in the relationship?

A. The third person is the one necessary for the fulfillment of the pattern which includes one of the persons in the dyadic marriage. (Also the other person in the dyadic marriage would require another person to complete another triad.) Envision a geodesic sphere with all those triangles on the surface. It is constructed of triangles. So in life, as people mature and develop, there comes a need for greater communion, larger expression, more growth. . . .

Q. And?

A. And so each person must develop his own relationships. They will be deeper and greater than the previous relationships but will also be inclusive of those relationships. They have to be inclusive: If you knock the props out of a structure you have to start all over again.

Q. Okay. Lets discuss the "triune marriage."

A. I don't like the word "marriage" there. The word that I use for the transcendent relationship is soul-mating, because marriage is different, you see, and came before. Soul-mating is more than marriage.

Q. Does not soul-mating also occur in the basic, dyadic marriage? Does not soul-mating first occur between the original partners, because there is a deep level of mutual Love and mutual trust for each other? This mutual Love and trust gives the partners the freedom to expand and fulfill themselves in wider more complex, interpersonal involvement. This necessarily occurs with people in the healing professions and other areas where complex human problems require depth of one-to-one involvement with persons outside the marriage. The soul-mating concept does not do away with the mutual responsibility of the partners to each other? Please explain the difference between soul-mating and marriage for me, then.

A. Well, I think, probably, at the beginning of a marriage, when two young people first come together that it is a type of soul-mating at the stage of their development at that time. So that this would be very similar. But as they grow and develop, and become more themselves and their identities are more firmly established, and have become one so that they are really one unit (one body in a way) and the marriage is consummated, that is, totally fulfilled, they are not to stop growing and developing. As they grow then, not away from each other but sort of through each other (like X-rays passing through matter) their universes are different but at the same time a circle around them. It is inclusive. As each person meets others, then, out in the world, they come to other and deeper relationships, communication, communion with other persons, that their increased psychic growth allows, partly because of the enriching experience of the marriage itself. They grow and become larger personalities. Then as each pespn meets complementary personalities to what he has become, (including his total marriage, family and other aspects of identity), the affinity between certain persons may result in soul-matings and may issue in many kinds of expression: social, vocational, artistic, sexual, and many others. There can be a total involvement of the individuals with each other, then, at this greater level, inclusive of the marriage, but not involved with it; not part of it.

Q. Okay. This is the point that is revolutionary in thought. Because of traditional theological, monogamous concepts then, I will ask you this question, How does this transcend the adultery problem?

A. Well, this is the hard part, for understanding and for action. The soul-mating should never occur until the marriage is completely fulfilled. Think of osmosis for instance, in plants or liquids. There is a flow between the two liquids from the denser to the less dense, until there

46

is a saturation level reached which is the same in both. When this occurs then the flow stops, and it needs to be reactivated by adding something to one or the other to unbalance the dead level. This is the same kind of thing that happens in human marriage. When that point is reached, another person very often enters the situation, but up until now this catalyst has most often caused disintegration and disruption. Ideally in the past, God in Christ fulfilled this requirement metaphysically. Or the children of the couple fulfilled this requirement, since life was short and fully occupied on a more physical level.

LOOK UP OSMOSIS IN ENCYCLOPEDIA

Q. I originally asked this question, "Is the third party God, or can the third party be another human being?"

A. Well, I think probably that I would say that the third party is God and then I would ask, "where is God?" Because of the incarnation, I feel that God is in people, at least in his most real relation to us as whole persons. And in order to Love God with all one's heart, soul, mind, and strength, one must love persons with all one's heart, soul, mind, and strength. Because if one does not love someone he has seen, in this way how can he love God whom he has not seen? (as Jeasus said.) So to learn to love God completely, one must learn to love human beings completely. The accomplishment of this is something that progresses. Now people will say, "This is what marriage should be". Yes, ideally, maybe, but people in the world are not ideal, and the thing that really happens is that two young people are not mature enought to be able to love with all their potential strength. They do not yet have all their potential, heart, mind, or soul . . . so the time comes, in order to love God fully with everything they have and are, greater personal relationships are required.

IMAGINE YOUR HEART IS A FUNNEL: DURING YOUR LIFETIME YOU PROGRESSIVELY POUR NEW LOVES INTO IT! THOSE AT THE BOTTOM HAVE BECOME PART OF YOUR BODY AND SOUL! NEW LOVES ARE ADDED ON TOP!

Q. Other than the original marriage partner?

A. Yes, partly because the original marriage partner is already totally included, and there is more.

Q. I heard you say that this third party can be another human being. I heard you say that this third party can be God. Or are you saying that it is always God? And in terms of the geodesic principle, this original dyad sometimes does not fulfill the total, cosmic potential, awareness, cosmic Love . . .

A. Well, you could say, NEVER does.

Q. Oh! Does, then, the second or triadic relationship fulfill it?

A. No. It doesn't. But after the triad is formed, there is a complete unit and any other relationships are outside it, either by individual or group. A triangle is formed. There is a completed structure. Other individuals must have a different, new relationship. The triad is the limit to this kind of relationship, (in case you are thinking of quadrilaterals, for instance.)

Q. This eliminates the communal marriage?

A. Right. The communal marriage is eliminated: I studied this experiment (from a distance) but it obviously eradicates spiritual freedom, that is, the interior affinity principle of the persons caught in it, besides eliminating the tensegrity necessary to the structure, which comes from the distance between persons, essential to fully living as individuals.

My great fear is that marriage, that great fundamental institution of the ages, will be undermined by this vision of larger spiritual affinities. Peter states "The passions of the flesh war against the soul". Our problem is that the passion of the soul requires the flesh! Love demands the total person. But this must include the two who have become one through natural marriage. This is where tensegrity and the structure concept enter in. The choices are made by the Spirit, the Creator, identifying the persons, and the holy, inner energies to be honored, never at the expense of, and always inclusive of, the natural marriage which is the base. Our guideline here is the Golden Rule (as it was originally stated) that is, in the plural and must be sensitively and thoughtfully applied. It is important to remember that if the natural marriage is not maintained at the highest possible level, the soul-mating relationship cannot be maintained either. It will either degenerate into adultery, by replacing the marriage, or disintegrate altogether. One of the intents of this paper is to undergird and support family life as it faces the changes that ARE taking place in society, and to show that marriage and family life are essential, as the base, to ever higher and more complex relationships of LOVE.

Q. Are you suggesting that a man and wife can arrive at a level of trust which would allow other sexual relationships and still maintain the basic marriage?

A. Soul-mating, in human community, seems to be required by the process of life toward its goal. The purpose of life, as I see it from the observations I make of history (and existantial being) is that existence and growth transcends physical sex toward complex unity of everything that is, or that is to be. Sexual relationships may happen, but—this complex creation moves constantly toward greater organization and higher consciousness. The ultimate result of this dynamic process being a universe totally organized, totally complex, and totally conscious. Total complexity includes eternal life, obviously. (To be total everything that has been or can be must be incorporated into it.) The "passage of time" does not destroy that which it apparently passes. In the fabric of infinity, complexity of structure brings about total consciousness. Whatever we can achieve of "more being in greater union" contributes to this "end". Faithful to each and inclusive of all, Faceted Love. Timing and Social Structure, by true inner affinity, must be developed.

A pre-existent, totally conscious "Point" inseminates for birth (by permeation and cohesion) the great complexity, which in turn becomes, by degrees, totally conscious. (The Second Coming.)

The beginning of this great, essential task is to put Love under the control of the mind: in time, regulated; in space, confined and expressed. And having kept all natural explosions of it restrained and incidental, harness it to the purpose of God to unite all things in their proper place and order, replacing the chaos in human events with the beautiful timing and order of the galaxies. For highest development and crowning glory, humanity is now required to accept, tame, and control the primary cause of creation; Love. Bringing all things into perfect subjection, and accepting the suffering and mistakes of this labor to become children of the Living God, in the name (nature) of the pioneer of Love, Jesus the Christ, perfectly individual, perfectly united, all in One in order.

$$\triangle \heartsuit <$$

In considering the Spiritual ordering of Love, we come upon the problem of adultery. Jesus said that divorce is adultery. Adultery is the substitution of one person for another. So what is a better way? We must accept the Spiritual ordering of human sexuality in which the lower levels of life are included in the development of something new. If the patterns of marriage and freedom are to be embraced together, we must resolve this traditional confict between marriage and freedom. Jesus also said that to be lured by passing physical attractions is adultery. We cannot build on the shifting sands of casual relationships. I think he was still talking about this when he gave his famous teaching about cutting off a hand or digging out an eye.

God is Love, the Spirit consciously creating the Earth and the universe, giving life to matter, and to Love a soul. We Love on the natural, social level according to currently accepted standards and customs. We should realize that loving on the spiritual level requires the material, all of it, of which we as persons are made. To live in the larger world with someone who has been drawn to us by maturity of identity is to know the Power which is continuing the creation in the complex development of the universe.

Q. Are you implying that we can no longer be "hung up" on sex as Love?

A. Right. Love is the Cause. Sexual expression may or may not be a result.

Society is coming, more and more, to understand the necessity of specialization for complexity and wholeness. This is especially true in the specialization of spiritual affinities, which is where the action is. The world must achieve these one to one structural relationships besides living in great universal and fluid good will. (Agape).

For a stable social structure undergirding homes, institutions, and nations with peace and contentment, we must overcome our taboos of centuries and generations past, and accept the new Spiritual ordering of life, which does not annul natural law but transcends it with inclusive Love. Buckminster Fuller says,"Structure is triangle." Human fulfillment requires soul-mating, beyond the natural marriage and/or family unit. A social structure must be built into an edifice which gives the spiritual values of Love and growth preeminence over all natural encumberances. But loyalty and faithfulness are Spiritual values. Therefore we must learn differentiated, and inclusive Love.

Love draws us unto deep, high, timed, ordered expression, resulting in the ecstacy of union and the agony of sacrificial action. Love is obedient to the "Spirit which blows where it will". The two activities of uniting and sacrificing continue until the final consummation of all things.

Those who sow to the flesh reap death and decay; those who — sow to the Spirit reap eternal infinte Life!
- SEE GALATIANS 6:8

Marriage, or the equivalent, comes first. "First the flesh and afterward the Spirit".* Marriage is a basic biological reality. Soul-mating is a basic, Spiritual reality. Love is like osmosis. The Spirit flows between two people in Love until they become one flesh, When this density level is reached a transfusion is required to stimulate the flow and activate growth. The complexification of social structure is necessary to an increase in human consciousness. This must be accomplished by Spiritual timing and ordering. So, on the natural level, (which comes first) we have Love and marriage. Later, an outgrowth of spiritual development and affinities; Love and soul-mating. This is one of the tensegrity factors of human life. Timing is important and balance maintained until death.

The beautiful picture of holy Christian families, living together in a fireside-glow kind of love and fellowship, making up churches, as colonies of Heaven, and eventually Heaven itself, is an infantile vision. Soul-mating, in the matrix of Spiritual affinities, must be included by the High Community where free persons obedient to the Spirit, are neither domesticated nor controlled by human reason and convention, alone. The eternal triangle is a Spiritual mystery challanging man's greatest capacity to Love.

Providence, in coincidence, has created the universe, and now seeks to perfect humanity in freedom and order, inclusive. What other accomplishments may follow from this single step forward, no one can say. Consider that it was less than one hundred years from the horse and "buggy" to the moon! And we didn't even want to go! "The very thing man did not think could happen, is what God has prepared for those who Love Him" (1 Corinth. 2:9)

You must Love the Lord your God with all your heart, mind, soul, and strength in a person, for intensity, and in the whole creation for fulfillment, through Christ, the Truth, the Way, and the Life. Jesus gave us one new commandment: "Love one another"........totally, sacrificially, creatively, specifically! Love draws, intensifies, develops, and perpetuates identity. The highest and most inclusive Love can only occur with the fulfillment of individual potential. We do not evaporate into Love! A great Love includes matter, life, and all previous relationships in the new concentration.

When all the potential in a natural marriage and community has been realized the soul reaches out for more Love and more Being. But such growth is improbable if divorce has separated the natural units. (Even as death separates the cells of a body). The eternal triangle is the basic, structural unit necessary for the continued development of humanity. If we do not achieve this level of Spiritual maturity, the whole structure will collapse and some other life form will arise which is able to continue the growth of the universal Consiousness of Love.

Many never arrive at this specialization of Love in this life-time. But soul-mating is being required of more and more people, who do not know what is happening to them, or what they

* St. Paul

50

must do to fulfill their responsibility in a positive way. A great Love is rarely perfected except among those who are sensitive enough to discriminate between sublimation (harmony and spiritual growth) and <u>adultery</u> (<u>substitution and disintegration</u>). These relationships, amoung other things, can be the means for eliminating dependency upon those terribly destructive substitutes for persons such as alcohol, drugs, and <u>things</u>.

△♡ <

Love is eternal. Life, eternal life, is the orderly functioning of complexity. The greater the complexity the greater the consciousness, according to Teilhard de Chardin. So that many parts may interact in continuous beauty, there must be the cohesive power called Love. More and more Love will bridge the gaps between conscious units until all are One, perfectly individual, totally Conscious, in dynamic union and communion.

In the metamorphosis of death, as in any other metamorphosis, it is the relationship of the parts to each other which remains constant, so that, for instance, <u>this</u> caterpillar becomes <u>this</u> butterfly and not a <u>different</u> butterfly. So relationship, Love, is essential to eternal identity Relationship is a component of complexity; as complexification and consciousness increase, "we shall know as we are known".

We must begin to build using both the natural and the spiritual facts of life. One of the spiritual facts of life is the "Eternal Triangle", The theme of most literature, music, art, and psychology! The complicator of human life! It holds the possibility of great structural strength for social stability and peace, if it is rightly understood, accepted, and used. While repressed and untamed, it causes disintegration and destruction by breaking out with uncontrolled violence, the raw power of loose life.

Someday, after mastering the winds the waves, the tides and gravity, we shall harness for God the energies of Love, and then, for the second time in the history of the world, man will have discovered fire".

—Teilhard de Chardin

Everything which is disintegration (death) by reconstitution must eventually be overcome within it.

The antidote to entropy is Love. Who, in the Body of Truth, is the conscious, complexifying "active ingredient". Love is the Alpha and the Omega. We are made by his cohesive power (Spirit), and in his Conscious Image, revealed in and by Christ.

NOTES:

Our goal is spiritual union so complete that physical union is incidental, and finally unnecessary. God, Love, within all is building Heaven here.

"Good news!
Liberty to captives!
Sight for the blind!
Freedom from oppression!"
Luke 4:18 — we, find
Is the Christs own Manifesto
For humanity, Love's leaven.
God's will is being done!
On Earth as it is in Heaven!
—LUKE 4:18

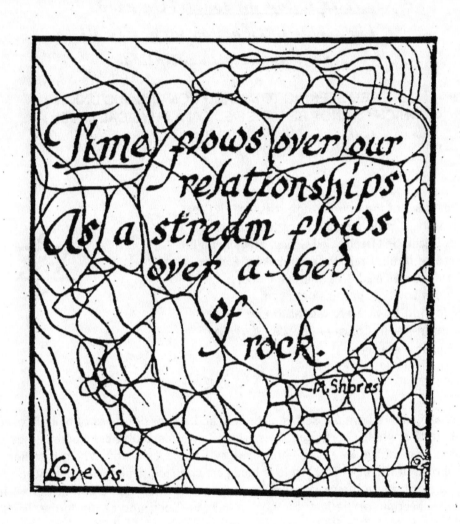

Time flows over our
relationships
As a stream flows
over a bed
of
rock.

—M. Shibras

Love is.

Identification in Eternal Life -
(SALVATION MEANS - ETERNAL IDENTITY)

It is union of souls We need.
The soul's satisfaction surpasses all
sexual and selfish satiation.

(WE ARE SEEKING TOTAL AND CONTINUOUS UNION
WHICH CANNOT BE SATISFIED ON A PHYSICAL LEVEL.)

☐ The message of the future is the message of <u>Great Love</u>.
So great there is no means of consummation
Except Death. Self-Death. Self-Giving, Suicidal LIFE!
Loving one in all: Great Pain,—and Great Elation.
Unselfed,—Spirit Filled,—All Boundaries Burst,
The soul's Love-Life in transformation;
One life lived as we were meant to Live
From Birth ——To Cross——To Life: *Love!*
Our Human Destination.

☐   In all genuine Love the self is shattered, and a consciousness of being broken, only a fragment of a whole, is <u>realized</u>. In spiritual Love this brokeness continues as a lifelong vocation, demanding unceasing effort to draw the pieces of the Whole together, in order to heal oneself within it. The World is being created (redeemed) be Love. Beyond the coupling of marriage, in the triad, (and the progression of organic union in Christ) how conscious we become of the fact that Love requires a Body, and of the further truth that this mortal one is not adequate to express Love in completeness. A great Love requires a larger body. No person is equal to the call of all the infinite demands of Love. But Love demands expression; the larger Body is the only answer. So we find other parts of the Body in grouping by inner affinities, in the spirit given through Christ by God for our comfort, and the fulfillment of Love. "Comfort one another". This can only be done on the spiritual level inclusive of the physical, in faithfulness to triune Love, that the order, power, and glory of Love may be consummated in the Earth.

MAKE ALL THINGS NEW

The simple truth we always fight,
The "Eternal Triangle" is right!

Without it architecture falls,
It braces great cathedral walls.

We are so stubborn, hard and slow
When it comes to truth that makes us grow.

"That which is born of the flesh is flesh,
That which is born of Spirit, spirit.".

The call is to INCLUSIVE LOVE.
Are we able, now, to hear it?

No substitution, adulteration,
But Spirit ordered love-relation.

The chaos of multiple mating rejected;
The beauty of triune-love perfected.

New structure - - - that we may be given
Faithfulness to home and Heaven.

We are divided. To become whole
We must make of two loves, with body and soul,

One life. Which is free from our tribal past
And in the mould of the future cast.

We must carefully pray our particular part
In the symphony played by the Infinite Heart.

"Love alone," wrote Teilhard de Chardin, "is capable of uniting living beings in such a way as to complete and fulfill them, for it alone takes them and joins them by what is deepest in themselves."

Christ alone is capable of uniting persons in such a way as to complete and <u>fulfill</u> them, for his spirit, alone, joins them by what is <u>deepest</u> in themselves.

— Maryann Shores

READ HIS OWN WORDS.
WHAT DID HE REALLY SAY?

CHRIST BY TORCHLIGHT, ON THE NIGHT HE WAS BETRAYED

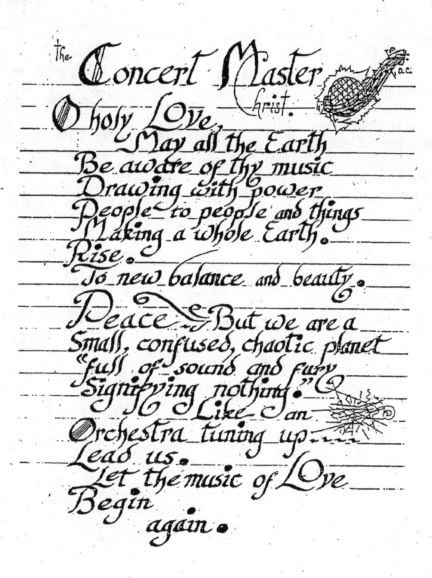

The Concert Master
Christ. a.c.

O holy Love,
    May all the Earth
Be aware of thy music
Drawing with power
People to people and things
Making a whole Earth.
Rise.
    To new balance and beauty.

Peace — But we are a
small, confused, chaotic planet
"full of sound and fury
Signifying nothing."
        Like an
Orchestra tuning up.
Lead us.
    Let the music of Love
Begin
    again.

WHY DO I LOVE YOU?
YOU LIGHT UP MY LIFE
YOUR EYES WINDOWS
FOR MY SOUL.

Love is Wise.

WRITE A POEM ABOUT LOVE.

LOVE IS WISE

Love is the Spirit
Which draws together
Proverbial birds
Of proverbial feather!

Chin to fiddle
Apple to teeth
Finger to fur
Holly to wreath!

Atom to atom
Spirals and chains
Cells to cells
Joys to pains!

Nutmeg to doughnut
Eyes to eyes
That's how I know
That Love is wise!

Man to woman
Souls to mates
That's how I know
That Love creates!

Out from within
Emerging souls
Fragments and parts
Becoming wholes!

Love and truth
Can bring to birth
And save the whole
Unfinished Earth!

* * * *

Tendrils of being
Reach beyond
the trellis bars
For reflected
Light.

↑ _____ ↓
HAIKUS — 17 SYLLABLES

Hayden mem-
orized.
I am a memory
too!
Yours! a part
of you.
_____

The drawing power
Of your hidden Being
glows —
Until I am here.

The pool of Light
Follows the actor
Wherever he goes.
Light, my home.

* * * *

"Those places (at right and left) are for those for
whom they have been prepared by my Father."

—Jesus

* * * *

Source of rivers,
Washer of pebbles,
Comber of rivergrass,
Blower of foam,
Within and without me,
Recover, re-enter
Re-bear me
Home.

* * * *

ALL PROGRESS IS TRANSGRESSION OF LAW. NOT
ALL TRANSGRESSION OF LAW IS PROGRESS!

* * * *

YOUR VERSE:

DISCOVERY

I comprehend you in the bareness
Unbeautiful, unplanned.
All our unshared days are spanned
By awareness.

The Whole has come in us
As emptiness is filled;
A symphony I heard
Reverberates unstilled
As it would not do
If I had heard
That symphony with you.

Nothing comes between us.
So much nothing! Complicates.
By our living it creates
A consciousness of Love.

Outside, no universe I see.
I bring to you the universe to be.

* * * *

See the soul Within.
The blending Light thus strikes
Through flesh
To distant Star.

* * * *

Her heart caught
On a stalactite of truth
In his deep cavernous gaze.

* * * *

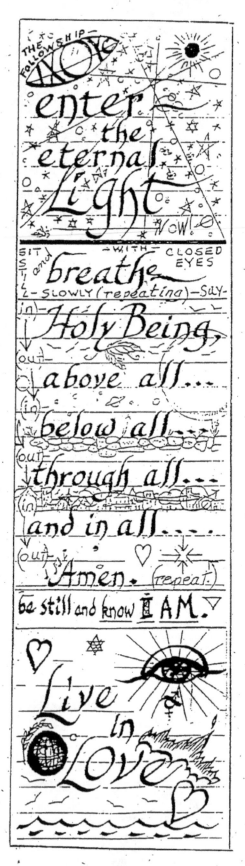

Book Mark

O Conscious Love

O Conscious Love in all things, drawing, binding,
Creating atom, star, and leaf and bird.
Who draws the soul to other souls in finding
A self emerge within the holy word.
A Conscious Love, you Spirit vainly brooding
Over Earth and flesh, for lasting joy & peace,
Who frees and binds (each stage of life including)
And runs before in passionate release!
O Conscious Love, you Spirit drawing leading
Complex order, world of beauty, on
Until all love inclusive and proceeding,
On triune Love become eternal Dawn!

Christ is born, without any violation of nature's laws, in the heart of the world...we feel we have the strength to raise up and perfect the world...In all things we are in communion with God whose power we make our own and whose encompassing Presence we intensify...powerful enough to turn each and every particular evil into good.

—Teilhard de Chardin
Writings in Time of War

In dying—we are born into infinite life.

*SING TO THE TUNE: O Perfect Love.

Shalom

He has risen.

— and we have already passed from death to life (-in-Love.)

Truly — and certainly I say to you, if anyone keeps my words he shall never see death.

— John 8/51

Love. According to God's purpose, which he set forth in Christ, as a plan for the fulness of time, to <u>unite</u> all things in him, things in Heaven and things on Earth.

- Ephesians 1:10

Love, the cohesive Spirit eternal, <u>creates by uniting</u>, and <u>sustains identity in complexity</u>. From beginning to end there is <u>continuously more</u> and <u>higher consciousness</u>.

Now you are the body of Christ, and individually members of it.

- 1 Corinth.

☐ There is only one force <u>universal</u> enough and powerful enough to fuse humanity into a functioning organism. That is erotic Love. Which must be directed and inspired by the One Spirit, expressed in <u>new</u>, fulfilling, and contagious ways.

Recognition of the reality of the One mind through the practice of sharing truth, and corporate worship, among other things, is actually the flow of LOVE. <u>Scheduled</u> <u>Loving</u> replaces biological sex as the most fulfilling human experience; our next step toward salvation in the One Body. It is shared only when and where there is inner affinity, hence a structural sorting of persons by the Creator Spirit results in eager functioning at a higher, wholesome level. We realize our own many facets and needs for particular others, for completion of life in Love.

The three loves: agape, philia, and eros, torn apart by the ancient Greeks, are once again united, One LOVE, triune.

Love and Time

The Sabbath rest is an expression of Love, and is scheduled once every seven days. The regularity and structure of life depends upon scheduling. One of the most important things to schedule is time for Love. Since the discovery of time and space, with Galileo, more and more importance is placed upon synchronizing events and human activities. Our dependence, independence, and interdependence for maximizing our potential, should be structured in time.

Psychologists say that definite time periods should be scheduled for, private communication with one's spouse, and with each child, separately, as well as with all <u>together</u>. Recent research also shows the great value of time spent individually, with old people (as well as the small group activities) to help them maintain their own sense of identity.

So, in the practice of inclusive Love, in which persons are identified as unique and as having well defined relationships with each other, time allowed and scheduled for in-depth communion is important. One needs to anticipate and prepare for sublimation and fulfillment.

The Layers of Time

Whatever has been Loved
Is eternally related.
Time never really passes;
It is accumulated!

Time is getting thicker:
More is added every day.
Whatever enters living
Can never pass away.

Our actions — and our dreams
Are carefully snowballed!
Enfolded in the layers of time
To be totally recalled!

And tho' what we call death
Entails a change of state,
The melting of the snow
Just opens the flood-gate! ~

The Eternal Now

Everything we are
Is all at once; Set free!
And finally we know —
What has been must always be.

We were happy; we were
We are made of all our past —
All our life-time story
Is all at-once. — at last!

In our deepest depths
We eternally remember —
Every summer hour —
Every soft September!

All our minutes and our days
Include our loving, (and our hates)
Time never really passes
It just accumulates.

by Maryann Shores 1989

66

PUT AN "E" BY EXPERIENCES YOU HAVE HAD

Love is partly involuntary,
    like breathing, partly
voluntary, like long distance,
swimming. —
"Having loved his own
who were in the world,
he loved them to the end."
                    -John 13:1

The new direction of
evolution is in quality of
life. "Life is being
ordered - - - by its inner
affinities."
                    -Tielhard de Chardin

What is constant in
    metamorphosis?
only relationship - - -
    (of the parts to
        each other.)
Love is eternal.

Our task is to help
the creation, and each
individual part of it,
to become *all that God
intends it to be.

*Altogether

U.C.C
-State Conference
1971

Providence in coincidence
has created the universe - -
and now seeks to
perfect humanity in
freedom and order.

For his highest development,
man is now required
to accept, tame,
and control Love—
To be perfectly individual,
perfectly united—
all in one in Order.

I pledge allegiance to the Earth,
One planet indivisible,
And to the Universe in which she lives,
One system, under God,
With freedom and fulfillment
For the highest life
And consciousness of all.

Jeremy Rifken's comment: "Every era rests its fortunes on a very few recitable aphorisms." Ours, necessary for a future, might be:

We pledge allegiance to the Earth; one planet indivisible.

WOMAN

How could she have known the bliss
Of the Holy Spirit's invasion
Would bring on unending travail?
Unending and total pervasion.
What will come has not before been.
What will come is some Other, New.
She shall not live to behold it,
But she knows that this Truth is True:
She has been taken and handled by God.
For what purpose she cannot say.
She only knows she must not fail
To give birth to the Light for the Day.

FRAGMENTS

LAWS OF LOVE - The laws which perpetuate Love. (Just as certainly functioning as the laws
of gravity.)

1. Enjoyment and fulfillment must be balanced by self-giving (even sacrificial) service to others
   by EACH, individually.

2. Love must not be ONLY a two way flow of magnetic energy between two. Gradually, "To whom
   much (LOVE) is given, of him shall much be required." Luke 12:48[b]

3. Involvement in creation and perfection of development is necessary for the continuous strength
   and ACTION of Love.

4. There is a STRUCTURE of life being built by Love, in which depth and faithfulness in a few
   relationships must balance good will and concern for ALL.

5. There must be a full acceptance of THE "FAMILY OF MAN," plus a SOUL-STRUCTURE for
   Eternal Love.

> I will pour out my Spirit upon all men.
> Your sons and your daughters will
>   prophesy;
> your young men will see visions,
> and your old men will dream dreams.
>   Acts 2:17[b]

MY STATEMENT OF FAITH - M. Shores

I believe that God is saving the whole Earth by uniting it in Jesus the Christ. The Structure of God is coming. It cannot be stopped: God overrules.

Love brings the right things together at the right time, creating first, matter, then life, then thought and soul. From pure energy electrons, protons, and neutrons form molecules. Molecules are brought together to form compounds. And compounds brought together in complex combinations have life. Living structures come together in specialized organization to become conscious. Consciousness in LOVE has soul: eternal identity and relationship.

Our bodies are terribly inadequate and temporary, but in some way express our essential selves, the units which will be joined to make a perfect whole. The complexity and beauty of the whole depends upon the full development of every person - each one irreplaceable by any other. All this coming together in order is LOVE: God, the beginning, permeating, cohesive Spirit, eternal.

The highest revelation of God is Jesus, Christ, and his "words are Spirit and Life".

The resurrection will be a wholly reconstituted creation. The fragments and elements being formed will find their perfection in union, in Christ, the incarnation effected by God - Who is Love.

He demonstrates for those who see
Eternal life-in-love to be
The truth, the way.
Love draws, intensifies, creates
The perfect whole: imperfect mates.
This is Love.
He overrules at whatever cost.
The whole is perfect; nothing lost.
God is Love!

GIVE ALL THAT YOU HAVE WITHIN YOU, AND EVERYTHING IS CLEAN FOR YOU.

Luke 11:41

Pray without ceasing-know the Tremendous Mystery.

70

ARRANGE
AN
EXPERIENCE
OF THIS
FACT

In the Church we really do go beyond sexual ultimates. We find a higher, holier, deeper, and more fulfilling experience in the Body of Christ. As a lover cherishes the parts of the body of the beloved, so we cherish all the other members of the Body of Christ, and find union in worship (and consecrated work). By dedication to the One, <u>identified for us in Christ</u>, we discover our union, (revealed in each others' eyes)! As we are arranged by truth in Holy relationship, there comes an awareness of Love and communion unequalled by any other act. Our souls are fused by a glance, <u>because the union actually preexisted in the Identified One</u>, and we have just been made <u>conscious</u> of that Love. "The eyes are the windows of the soul"... and our <u>Whole</u> Body is "full of Light."   —Jesus

<u>NOTES:</u>

What Soul is This?

(A THESIS IN SONG)

(may be sung to Greensleeves — very slow)

USE THIS RECITATIVE IN A GROUP

What Soul is this I recognize
Deep in the depths of certain eyes?
What flowing feeling, what liquid touch?
Who is this Person I Love so much?
This, this is the Holy One!
The Spirit blowing where He has gone!
This, this was in Jesus sent,
The Self-expression of what is meant!

to be sung

What flesh is this that looks like bread?
What food upon the Earth is spread?
What do I drink like water and wine?
What blood is flowing from your heart to mine?

spoken

This, this is the growing Son!
Divided among us to make us One!
Dismembered body, we seek our own;
Until there are none who can feel alone!

sung

What Love is this beyond my strength?
This drawing, drawing throughout my length?
What Love is this? By truth on fire!
This unfulfillable, dread desire?

spoken

This, this is the "Spirit of Truth"!
Who patterns our living of age and youth.
Who, if we follow we are not misled,
But find Love and a place we can pillow our head.

sung

What shall I do to Love as I should?
To ease the ache and bring the Good?
How be faithful, and full, and free?
And know all the Love that was meant for me?
Know, know that the world is One!
We are all one body beneath the sun!
Know, know that life is designed,
Each his particular Loves to find!

sung

Why, why, finding those called to me
Do I also find that Love is not free?
Why does it cost all I have become?
It includes the deaf, the deformed, and dumb?

spoken

Because, when the number is all complete,
And the Earth fulfilled in music sweet,
Eternal life-in-Love the dawn!
We will, altogether, be whole, and One!

sung

THE FUTURE OF LOVE

A space capsule appears to defy the law of gravity as it uses that law to overcome the original limitations of matter. Reorganization and order allows us to control gravity and fly beyond the capacities of birds. A Love that transcends greatly overcomes what is transcended.

△♡<

Prophecy:

Eventually there will be a social structure which allows real Love, recognizing its triangular form in microcosm as in macrocosm. It will include the family as a basic unit, reinforcing and sustaining it by being superimposed upon it, faithful to both the natural and the supernatural. The mysteries of Love will be respected, its ordering accepted, and its hazards avoided by complete submission to the consciousness (Truth) of the Living God. Much time will be spent in study, meditation and arranging a holy life in contact with God, obedient to Love. The Loves we now know are a foretaste of this Heaven to come, here and hereafter.

We must learn Eternal Love, the expanded life of controlled and inclusive Love.

"WHAT GOD CREATED TO BE TOGETHER, MAN MUST NOT SEPARATE."..."THAT THEY MAY ALL BE ONE."

△♡<

My purpose, as a disciple of Christ, is the same as his: TO RECONCILE THE WORLD TO GOD IN LOVE.

Equal Rights
Have this mind among yourselves,
which you have in Christ Jesus, who though
he was a revelation of God, did not count
equality with God(!) a thing to be grasped,
but emptied himself, taking the form of a
servant. —*Phil 2:5-7*

△♡<

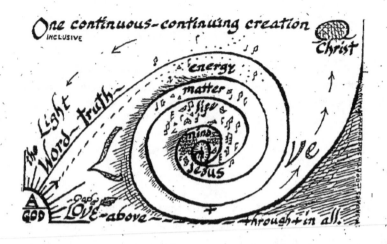

One continuous-continuing creation
INCLUSIVE
Christ

the Light
Word-truth
energy
matter
life &
mind
Jesus
Love
God
Love-above
through + in all.

MAKE
A FOIL
OR
PAPER
MOBILE

The Movement of Love

I. Self-centered Love (descending spiral). The fervent desire to satisfy self by direct union with another person. Direction of movement of exclusive Love, results in: Selfcenteredness, isolation, jealousy, disillusionment, despair and suffering—finally driving one to the voluntary actions of Love No. II. ➤

The intensity of this Love is necessary for genuine experience of altruistic Love, which comes from realizing that total, self-other Love is impossible without including the whole.

II. God-centered Love (ascending spiral). The fervent desire for and expression of the greatest good for another and all. Self-forgetting. The direction of movement of self-giving, all inclusive Love results in: exalting ever-increasing life, community, joy, newness, creativity, growth and fulfillment.

◄ But this love is not real without love No. I, necessary for identity and structure of eternal life-in-love, which depends upon sustained relationships, and an identified self. Alternate love experiences seem to be necessary.

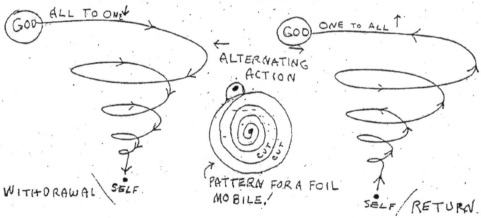

GOD   ALL TO ONE
ALTERNATING
ACTION
GOD   ONE TO ALL

WITHDRAWAL   SELF.
PATTERN FOR A FOIL MOBILE!
SELF/RETURN.

READ
HUMAN
ENERGY
By
Teilhard

from HUMAN ENERGY by Teilhard de Chardin. (pp. 32-34)

"Hominized (humanized) Love is distinct from all other love, because the "spectrum" of its warmth and penetrating light is marvelously enriched. No longer only a unique and periodic attraction for purposes of material fertility; but an unbounded and continuous possibility of contact between minds rather than bodies the play of countless subtle antennae seeking one another in the light and darkness of the soul; the pull toward mutual sensibility and completion, in which preoccupation with preserving the species gradually dissolves in the greater intoxication of two people creating a world. It is a fact, that through woman the universe advances toward man. The whole question (the vital question for the earth) is that they shall recognize one another.

If man fails to recognize the true nature, the true object of his love, the confusion is vast and irremediable. Bent on assuaging a passion intended for the ALL on an object too small to satisfy it, he will strive to compensate a fundamental imbalance by materialism or an ever-increasing multiplicity of experiments............

If only man would <u>turn and see</u> the reality of the Universe shining in the spirit and through the flesh........In this sense, man can only attain woman by consummating a union with the Universe."

HOW LOVE SAVES THE WORLD

1. When two persons fall in Love, nothing is as important to them as that Love.

2. They discover certain laws operative: Love must be totally exclusive and totally inclusive at the same time.
   a. Love for one must be deep, high, total and EXCLUSIVE.
   b. Love for others must be impartial, equal, balanced and INCLUSIVE.
   c. Love requires a common focus for continuation. (Given in Christ).
   d. This Love requires eternity/infinity for its perfection.
   e. The purpose of Love is cohesive structure.
   f. "Structure is triangle"—Buckminster Fuller.
   g. And perfects the Earth for fulfillment and identity in relationships of Love, exclusive and inclusive.
   h. "The passions of the flesh war against the soul".

THE PASSION OF THE SOUL REQUIRES THE FLESH.

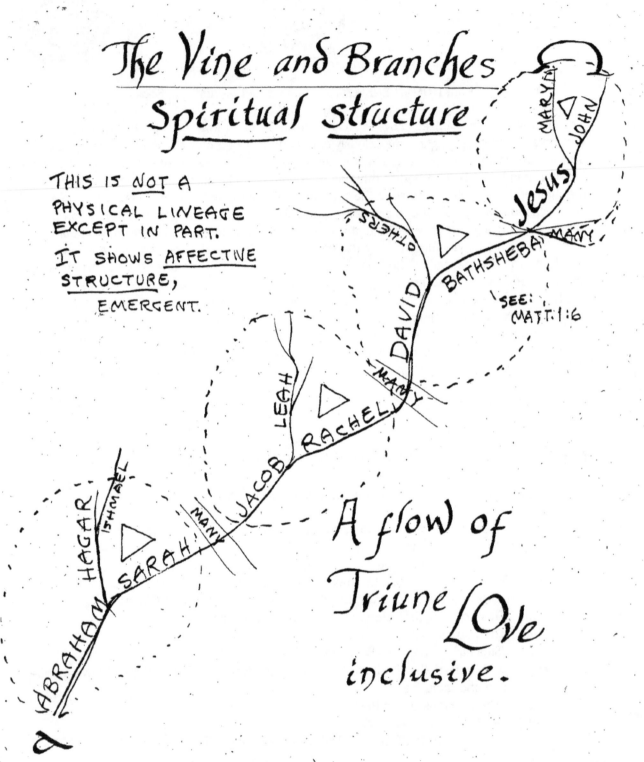

The Vine and Branches
Spiritual structure

THIS IS NOT A
PHYSICAL LINEAGE
EXCEPT IN PART.
IT SHOWS AFFECTIVE
STRUCTURE,
    EMERGENT.

MARY
JOHN

JESUS

OTHERS

BATHSHEBA MARY

DAVID

SEE:
MATT. 1:6

MANY

LEAH
RACHEL

JACOB

A flow of
Triune Love
inclusive.

ISHMAEL
HAGAR

SARAH
MANY

ABRAHAM

TENSEGRITY THEOLOGY

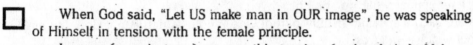

☐ When God said, "Let US make man in OUR image", he was speaking of Himself in tension with the female principle.

In man (generic term) we see this tension (and polarity): Male and female; right and left; good and evil; life and death.

The Earth is also created in "their" image, expressing both unity and disintegration. Simplistic example: The Light is modified in matter. God overcomes this by complexification. Life emerges. There is grass. The Destroyer produces, (complexified by God's Life-Force,) the insect. Which is eaten by the bird! Which is eaten by the cat! Which is killed by the fox! Which is killed by man! Who is absorbed into the collective! It is as though God cannot prevent the Destroyer's action, but he can complexify and overcome it by integrating it into the next level of Life.

What is the ultimate interaction? Ultimate interaction, overcoming, ordering, complexification has no end. But occurs in time. Time does not pass, it accumulates specifics.

☐ The uncreated God (the "I AM" or Being) became a Person in One man, and is becoming that Person in humanity. The whole inseminated creation is involved. It is evolving as God overcomes disintegration with complex unity. The continuous unification and re-unification of chaos is accomplished by Love, the drawing Power of Light.

The highest that humans can know of complexity is Person. The Seed, (the Son) and consciousness growing in the Earth is opposed by all the forces of destruction. There are wars. There are demons and disintegrating persons which can only be redeemed by the ordering, reuniting Life. Love, therefore, continues to draw right things together. This is how the Seed-Person (Christ) saves the world. (John 3:17) god is uniting all things in him. (Eph. 1:10) Faithful, progressive, inclusive, identifying Love continues its mysterious action bringing "Life out of every form of death" (Teilhard), creating infinite variety. The darkness cannot put out the Light, but produces all the colors of the rainbow BY that Light. (And all the eels and barnacles; snakes and ostriches; butterflies and whales!)

△♡<

☐ The Bible expresses some of this dance of Life (caught by the minds of men,) in which the Word, like Life, is intermixed with absurdity. Truth and error intriguingly combined!

△♡<

☐ Since the beginning, there is more and more consciousness: 4 billion times Adam! The tension is terrific!

God does not rule, but overrules; a third act. In duality alone structure collapses. In more and more triune complexification, structure is built. (As Buckminster Fuller says, "Structure is triangle")

☐ We must _be_, altogether, the "Second Coming".
"Now, we are the body of Christ, and individually, members of it."—I Corinthians: 12:27
"It does not yet appear what we shall be."

So we are each a specific identity, part of One Whole, which is not God, but in which (and without which) He Lives.

> Mix the Earth until it all rises.
> Continuous fear produces irrational acts -
>   Strive to drive humanity sane.
>   "Practice evangelical non-violence."
> — Esquivel
> (Be Peace full, and creative.)

The Opposite of Love.

☐ We usually think of hate as the opposite of Love; because hate is the wish for a death. Psychologists say indifference is the opposite of Love, because it is non-Love. But Love itself is not a Word, or an emotion, or a wish, but the One Essential Reality: the Order, Power, and Glory forever. God is Love, conscious. (That is why Love always makes more aware.)

☐ Statement: Love, the cohesive spirit eternal, creates by uniting, and sustains identity in complexity. From beginning to end there is continuously more and higher consciousness.

☐ God is and is becoming. He is the essence in the All. Imagine _infinite_, ordered, complexity. We Love "According to God's purpose which he set forth in Christ as a plan for the fulness of time, to unite all things in him, things in Heaven and things on Earth."—Eph. 1:10. Jesus' life and words grant eternal Life—specific identity-in-relationship forever. He came to bring (what everyone really wants more than anything else) Eternal-Life-in-Love. We are to be conscious of our identities in our relationships forever.

WITHOUT JESUS, THE CHRIST, EVERYONE MAKES GOD IN HIS OWN IMAGE.

☐ There is no real Love when God's revelation of himself (in Jesus the Christ) is not realized. It takes the continuous, electric flow of magnetic power from the True, living God to hold things in their proper orbits. "Seek first the Order of God and all these things shall be added." Love will sustain, envelope, and fulfill you: Love is only glimpsed or ends in despair in ANY OTHER WAY.

△♡<

☐ When spiritual communion occurs, biological indulgence must be controlled to maintain the power, prevent destruction of higher values, and allow freedom of expression to the Holy Spirit. Real, suffering Love forces prayer and is a SPIRITUAL PROCESS not to be grounded in the flesh. We must carry the Current.

△♡<

☐ It is true we suffer from separation, but the way to close the circuit is absolute obedience to the highest we know, day by day.

△♡<

CON-SOULATION

☐ There is an uneasy and ever increasing drive toward unity in the human race (which, itself, has not yet discovered that the means is neither flesh nor conformity). The situation must be resolved spiritually, by intense attention and dedication in every activity and function to the Consciousness of God, present in Truth. Through obedience to Him (see Jesus) there is a breakthrough for Love. This will bring true union and order among individuals according to Divine law and design.

△♡<

☐ "Holiness is a preoccupation with the reality of Ultimate Good."

△♡<

☐ This is not a "post-Christian" age but the externalized Christian age where instead of trying to reduce life to "spiritual things", it is recognized that the Essence (like salt) is free and permeating all that is. That salt is Love. But if it has lost its flavor how can you season anything with it? LOVE MUST BE WITHOUT PRETENSE.

△♡<

☐ You cannot truly Love an abstract God. If you do not Love a person whom you have seen, you cannot Love God whom you have not seen?

△♡<

☐ Without the passion of erotic Love we cannot learn total sacrifice; self-giving. We must continuously Love to take up our cross daily. That is why even "if we give our bodies to be burned, or give all our goods to feed the poor, and do not have Love" we have not found the Way.

△♡<

☐ The Way
Of suffering Love.

Distance:........
Time.................
God's design.

Familiar
With death.
Overcome.

Take up your cross daily
And follow.....................
The Way
Of Suffering:
LOVE.

△♡<

☐ Love is an aching, drawing emotion which, if rightly used results in something like the induction method of learning in us. The Love object is God extended in the personalities he calls to us. There is a continuity to life intended to run through flesh and spirit; birth and rebirth, marriage; soul-mating, and even death.

△♡<

MARRIAGE AND LOVE

☐ Soon after marriage repulsion and separation begin in a rather rhythmical pattern so that it takes effort and self-sacrifice to hold it together. We develop strength to maintain the marriage, at the same time finding ourselves in new spiritual relationships in society. When the Spirit stirs in the individual its force is divisive and a threat to the natural marriage unit. Unless we limit life to mutual idolatry, persons will grow and develop relationships with others.

CAN
A
MARRIAGE
BE
IDOLATRY?

80

Socially we find spiritual relationships in the order and arrangement that God, as Love, brings. "Those who are considered worthy to attain that life are neither married nor given in marriage but are like the angels of God."—Jesus. Spiritual growth occurs by the discipline of marriage on the natural level and discipline of obedience on the supernatural level. We trust God for the INCLUSIVE ORDER which provides FAITHFULNESS to each, and FREE-DOM for Love, to All.

△♡<

☐ We have one (already answered) prayer: Establish our Loves forever.

△♡<

☐

METHODS OF EXPRESSING LOVE

Biological. (Sexual expression and maternal instinct.)
Physical. (Ordinary work and athletics)
Mental. (Thought, word, and premeditated deed.)
Emotional. (The arts. All the categories mix and overlap.)
Spiritual. (The total persons dedicated to the One God and Whole neighbor. This is ordinarily experienced as worship. Mutual worship of God is the highest expression and experience of Love and may include any or all of the previous categories!)

△♡<

☐ "What good is life without Love?" "He who sows to the flesh will reap death and decay." He who sows to the Spirit will reap eternal Love, Identity, and community.

△♡<

☐ We must lift the lowest and most ordinary acts of life to the level of worship and dedication.

△♡<

☐ We cannot Love impartially because we are partial, parts of a Whole. But we must Love totally with what we are, and inclusively where we find ourselves. The variety in relationships is part of the pattern.

△♡<

☐ Sometimes, rising and doing what one most ardently wishes not to do results in peace and satisfaction. Life does not consist in prohibition of action, but in valiantly going forward against the greatest inertia, comfort, or complacency to DO what one is called to do. And we cannot even wait for the Spirit before we act. We go out each day without knowing where we are going. All our desires and all our needs completely subjected to the God of Love working in us.

81

LOVE IS REAL

In Love, how terribly dependent we realize ourselves to be upon God and upon whomever he calls to us in affinity of being.

The intention of Love is that people may live in Heaven here and hereafter, conscious of Love; absolutely and continuously led by his Spirit. All in life, and Love, and peace together, through Jesus, Truth, the self-expression of God, whereby continuous life, Love and union are possible. There is no other means of consummation for humanity.

THE GATE

"The gate is narrow and the way is hard that leads to life and few there are who find it".—Matt. 7:13-14.

The hard way: neither self-indulgence nor harsh repression, but obedient self-giving Love, Carefully true to oneself and the Highest. This is the agonizing life of tension and growth found in real Love, led by the Spirit, always failing of perfect expression, rising and rising again to try as long as life lasts to spend the body in the life of inclusive Love.

KALEIDOSCOPE

There's something about the Order,
The pattern's symmetry
Through which one gets a message
Of the Spirit, Holy, Free.
Divine Order takes the fragments
Of every day's few hours
And patterns them, whatever comes,
Arranging cosmic powers.
Galaxies and comets
In brilliant constellation!
All things, together, beautiful.
In silent orchestration.
Each confused and complex day
Becomes a new design!
No two days ever the same,
But each eternally mine!
So our lives and Loves and time
God does, himself, arrange.
Oh keep us in thy purpose,
Thy ways. (Thy peace, how strange.)

☐ As Jesus indicated in his description of the Kingdom as the sorting of the fishes of "all kinds", LIFE ITSELF IS A SORTING PROCESS. We are sorted, arranged by mutual affinities, resulting from our spiritual developments, find each other and establish eternal relationships. (That which is bound on Earth shall Be bound in Heaven"). The "Gospel" is this: GOD OVERRULES. Every fault and lack of life is being overcome.

△♡<

☐ We have the command to heal the whole world of its sickness, misery, and need. We can do this only by filling it FULL of LOVE, the Spirit that was in Jesus the Christ. Let this, thy will, be done through us, by us, in us, and to us, oh God!

△♡<

☐ Universal problem: How to find the right and sufficient expression for Love. One which rewards with the satisfaction that sexual expression gives but which when selfishly indulged, is spiritually abortive and produces all kinds of terrible evil. Love must be faithful on the natural and super-natural levels at the same time. "GIVE ALL THAT IS WITHIN, AND LOOK!, EVERYTHING IS CLEAN FOR YOU! -Luke 11:41.

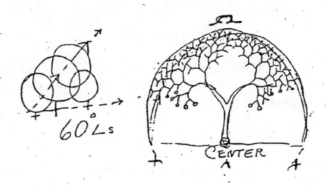

TRIUNE Love is beyond anything we can yet begin to comprehend:
beauty, harmony and interaction; growth.
These relationships, are necessary to the coming of
the great unity.

△♡<

☐ God is Love, the Spirit consciously creating the whole universe, giving life to matter and a soul to life: eternal identity in relationship (the source of identity). The triangle is the basic structural unit.

Jesus is the lamp of God's light.

△♡<

The purpose of Love is structure, to unite all things in their proper place and order. (see Eph. 1:10) There is no real Love outside the Trinity. God's revelation of Himself and Truth in Christ, and his action in the Holy Spirit requires us to seek first the rule of Love, and be sustained, enveloped, delighted and fulfilled.

△♡<

"Someday, after mastering the winds, the waves, the tides, and gravity, we shall harness for God the energies of Love, and then, for the second time in the history of the world, man will have discovered fire." -Teilhard de Chardin

△♡<

No stated truth can be accepted as absolute truth to be universally applied, or even accepted by the same person in similar situations, God's immediate guidance, ("Blessed are those who <u>hear</u> the word of <u>God</u> and do it"), takes precedence over all rules and formulated behavior patterns; the instant law is <u>Love</u>.

△♡<

Doing what comes naturally is entropy; doing what comes spiritually is life eternal. The very definition of life is Love: the continuous integration and organization of parts. First there is matter, then complexity, then life, then consciousness, then soul. Love brings INCLUSIVE progression.

△♡<

Progression is necessary: Nature rules; God overrules. Every lack of life is being overcome by this process. Love requires all the previous levels of life to create something NEW!

△♡<

Man's duality is resolved in trinity. We are held together and apart for our individual identity, by God Triune. Only Spirit builds the triad.

△♡<

Love, God present, takes precedence over law, God's past. The drawing power of the living God continues to work in us: First, a person becomes integrated: one person. Second, two persons become one in marriage. Third, three become a larger one, through soul-mating. Cohesive structure also occurs in groups, families, churches, etc.

△♡<

It took humanity centuries to learn that Love is trinity, triad, triune.

〰️⦿ᔭ♡ △▽─✡

....................and must have heart, mind and soul in tune, INCLUSIVELY.

△♡<

Two party, exclusive marriage is not complete, Abraham ("Father of our faith") had two wives'. Jacob (later called Israel) lived out the ordinary progression of human Love as it is usually (except for divorce) attempted, having married first Leah and then Rachel....

△♡<

Simple marriage of two persons, IF IT DOES NOT GROW, congeals both parties at the level at which they were united. It is flat because it is only two dimensional! Casual affairs and promiscuous relations disintegrate persons and lose Love because the Center is not fixed. Faithful and inclusive Love opens life, because it is not a comfortable dead end, but demands a great deal from the individual persons involved.

△♡<

It is important to keep the "corners" apart. Tensegrity = structure. The eternal triangle is in the Divine plan: Love and freedom. "For freedom Christ has set us free." This freedom and structure is the new social mandate for the perfection of humanity. And for the peace and development of the Earth. "That they may all be one."-Jesus

△♡<

THE PERSONAL DIMENSION

"Hurry! There is not much time to change the behavior that will save this planet" -Paul Ransom.

△♡<

The only POWER available, in common, to all people, is erotic Love. This Love must be shown to be our common denominator, and in its highest form, our hope.

△♡<

The secret of Love is to be always "in Love" with One, and to carefully protect and nourish that Love, while at the same time, giving to every other the same quality of Love. The same Love, really, flowing from that Source but differently expressed according to the needs of each, building the harmony and perfection of the whole world.

ARE WE LIVING A DIVINE PROCESS

Part one: HOW CAN I BLESS YOU

How can I bless you?
Isn't Love the way
To give you everything I am,
Share all I have?
No, this must be wrong:
The pain is great, and deep, and long.
How can I bless and leave you
Whole and strong?
How can I bless you?

I will pray with every breath I take
And dedicate each move I make
To fulfillment of the Master's plan
When Love shall be more possible for man.
But I cannot bless you.
(And I have a broken heart;
In this life we'll always be
Too far apart.)

Marriage is, on nature's plane,
What our spirits seek in vain.
There is no way for two to be one: whole,
Until the All, in union, makes one Soul.
And so we struggle on to fit the pieces true
Into the pattern of the order Coming through.

Part two: HOW DO I LOVE YOU NOW?

I Love you, with all the action of my life.
With every rising to perform a painful duty.
I Love you with the ache of rain at night,
And every sense of finding too much beauty.
Upon waking.....in the fuzziness of mind
That is there from childhood's ancient dreams.
I Love you as the one who brought me God
And the hope of life, (and death as it sometimes seems.)
I Love you as the Light. The flame is blue!
And shines in your eyes when God is near.
I Love you with involuntary breathing,
And endurance of the cross.....year after year.
I Love you with the Love beyond all time and place
Yet find that matter is the means,
As Christ found necessary flesh,
To build the simple sacraments and scenes
That establish an eternal growing pattern,
The complexity of human life to move.
I Love you in this way and all ways
To trust both you and God, Eternal Love.

beyond law and nature.
The same Love which holds all things
together at every level of creation.

People sometimes think that the great compassion which gives itself for humanity, the face-

People sometimes think that the great compassion which gives itself for humanity, the faceless whole or for a group (orphans or a segment of the poor) is the most Christ-like Love. But one does not really know Love until one has suffered in Love for an individual, (an intense and total Love) over a long period of time. Discovering one's absolute dependency upon another's personal act, learning vulnerability and mortality by experiencing human inadequacy and inability in the face of time, and the limitations imposed by space. Then with the anguish and ecstacy of Love one may learn to Love the ALL, others, or another, and God with a real, (still partial) Love of which humans are capable.

WHICH STAGE OF LOVE ARE YOU IN?

One cannot at first Love "others" when one is "in Love". However, later on, Love reveals the Whole, and the real needs of people become more apparent. Voluntary service becomes more humble, less conceited. One's commitment to Jesus' Way and God of Love, is more complete because of the continuous experience that nothing else really matters. That to "seek the Kingdom first" is actually the only way to find fulfillment for a Love which cannot be consummated because of its infinite and eternal dimensions! The individual persons are not adequate for a great Love

So "Our faith is in Him who brings life out of every form of death". -Teilhard de Chardin

And why not ?? God's principle observable activity is bringing order out of chaos. Death is disintegration (which simply means coming apart). Separation is a little death. Life is integration; coming together more and more and more.

△♡<

The BODY OF CHRIST (the Church) must prepare itself to BE the "Second coming of Christ".

△♡<

God is the Alpha and the Omega, the beginning and the end. In between is the Spirit and the process.

△♡<

Creation is progressing in individuation, and at the same time in unanimity resulting from common ideas, communications (tv) interests and desires. Beyond all these there rises the impulse to know and be known on a one to one spiritual basis, in the depth an intensity of a common involvement in God and His Kingdom of Love.

△♡<

Love All in one; Love One in all. This holds an extreme of faithfulness and a Spiritual security which could replace our vanishing material security-sense.

△♡<

Earth Song: Maybe we are beginning to hear the folk-forming music of the sphere.

△♡<

88

☐   It is our task to set life free from all the chains that bind it and to continue evolution toward the highest achievement in thought and action, through the Holy Spirit. Jesus is the Word; we are the music!

$$\triangle \heartsuit <$$

☐   You can live in Heaven here by making a Heaven here for those around you!

$$\triangle \heartsuit <$$

☐   Until the parts are perfectly developed and complex individuals, the Whole cannot be perfect.

$$\triangle \heartsuit <$$

☐   Soul-mating of the matured person to another completed soul can be the result of a good marriage and family life.

$$\triangle \heartsuit <$$

☐   The "naked ape" streaks to God! Let our christian life reveal 2000 years of spiritual growth: LOVE.

$$\triangle \heartsuit <$$

☐   I pray for continuously perfected complexity and consciousness: eternal identity in relationships of Love.

$$\triangle \heartsuit <$$

☐   The new social structure of human triads will result in harmony, peace and development undreamed of by our present chaotic, dualistic society.

$$\triangle \heartsuit <$$

NOTES:

☐   What happens to a cell when it becomes part of a higher organism? It specializes, and harmonizes. It "super-cooperates" (Teilhard) and that is Love!

△♡<

NEW YEARS GOALS

1. Life-is too short. We must lengthen it; reverse the aging process.
2. There are too many human limits. We must:
    a. develop persons
    b. correct obsolete laws and conventions.
    c. cultivate complex structure and mind.
3. There is too little time. We must use and order it by the Spirit of Jesus, LOVE, (and dance the music of life together.)
4. There is too much disorder and chaos. We must order all of life by Love, absorbing the Holy Spirit by reading the Words of Christ, himself, for his attitude.
5. Matter is subject to spatial limits and disintegration. We must help Love build the Earth by inner affinities: Heaven here and hereafter, Spiritual structure fulfilling Earthly needs and producing eternal life. Together, the Whole must be made of infinitely complex and perfected order, our individual identities and relationships guaranteed but perfected. See: Eph. 1:10....1st Corinth. 12:27 and Luke 21:27-28.

LIST NEW GOALS

△♡<

☐   "Perfect honesty" reveals a lack of personal integrity!

△♡<

☐   Contemporary temptations: Smallness of self, interest and life.
    ☐ Over-indulgence (food, and all sensations)
    ☐ Sexual expression without Love.
    ☐ Lack of appreciation (all kinds)
    ☐ Neglect of Truth (all kinds)
    ☐ Lack of control, (activity by mind.)
    ☐ Lack of Control of <u>mind</u> by heart and soul.
    ☐ Easy acceptance of evil circumstances and acts.

△♡<

☐   Imagine the world as a living, breeding growing multiplying jig-saw puzzle!! Which must be continuously put together correctly. It is Love who draws each piece to its own place, eventually!

IDENTITY

Daily, determined,
Devout dedication,
The Way to specific,
Eternal relation.
Changeless identity
Basic and true:
I am what I am
Because I Love you!
You! Particular,
(Christ like heart)
Binding on Earth
Never to part,
By the sorting process
Of freedom, mature.
The Heaven that is
Through all time to endure.

△♡<

The Increasing frequency of affection in same sex orientation may simply be nature's solution to the problem of the pressure of over-population! A really neat solution! If one accepts inner affinity ("deep calls to deep") and the Spiritual ordering of society (by Love) here and hereafter, the physical sexual expression of the person is incidental. (And at the same time essential, in the same way that eating is incidental in living but essential to life.) - See, John -13:23, 19:26 and 21:7. Also 13:1[b]

△♡<

Growth is: First, lust for things to have and to hold (to become; physically).
Second, the lust for experience (to know and to be; mentally).
Third, one delights to turn life inside out and give all one is and has, everything! Realizing, finally, Heaven here, now, forever coming; in, through, and to ALL, TOGETHER.

△♡<

Lets say that someone gives you a beautiful piece of cake, and you eat it, bite by bite, all up. You digest it and assimilate it, and it becomes part of YOU. That is like marriage.

The whole process takes a while, but you can never eat THAT piece of cake again. You can eat another piece of cake. Love is like cake. It becomes part of you. The purpose of Love is to build up by assimilation of experience, the human, conscious person. "We are what we Love". But those who try to eat the same piece of cake over and over again are making a mistake!

The closer we are to God, the
closer we are to those who are close
to Him. —Thomas Merton

91

Jesus was <u>hated to death</u> by those he tried to <u>Love to life</u>. Parts of the New Testament itself are a reaction against his TRUTH.

"All have sinned"......Everyone must come again and again, repenting, because we are <u>already</u>, before everything else <u>imperfect</u>. We are partial; we are not whole. We seek "more Being in greater union". (Teilhard)

CHRISTMAS

What can I send you?
Reality wanes.
Awareness perceiving
Apartness with pains.
"If I were a shepherd,
I'd bring you a lamb".
What can I send you
Of something I am?

No need to "send you!"
We already are!
Eternal Love came
With the first Christmas Star!
Separation: illusion.
Drawn into One (Whole)
Our free will determines
Which two make one soul.

☐   Jesus said, "Why do you Love only those who Love you? Even the heathen Love those who Love them. But I tell you Love your enemies". He also said, "From now on (that is, after he had come) a man's enemies will be the members of his own household". "Love your enemies."

$$\triangle \heartsuit <$$

☐   We are all One. We are all won! Love draws and unites.

$$\triangle \heartsuit <$$

☐   The most important truth for our generation is the REALIZATION that all of nature/creation, in its evolution to higher and more consciousness, is not only being PUSHED, it is being PULLED, by Something that was there before we were: Not only pulled but pulled together in ever greater order, beauty, and complexity, the maximum of which is consciousness. The Essence is already here. The Second Coming is Coming NOW!

$$\triangle \heartsuit <$$

☐   Between Being and Knowing
There is confusion. Growing
From complexity to conscious One,
God is Loving, just begun.

$$\triangle \heartsuit <$$

☐   The DANCE OF LIFE is becoming structure: see atoms, molecules, matter and mind!

$$\triangle \heartsuit <$$

☐   Help people to see how the goodness in each of them continues, by Love, toward One: Unification. And how the evil in them disintegrates and is destroyed (being re-used according to the law of the indestructibility of energy, to build up the good). Every person is "sifted like wheat": the good is united to the good and the evil is dispersed for a time, like chaff.

$$\triangle \heartsuit <$$

☐   Children's story: Think of the world as a big blue and green Easter egg. Now, when an egg hatches, everything that is in the egg becomes part of the bird So everything on Earth becomes part of Heaven.

$$\triangle \heartsuit <$$

☐   God's will is LOVE: discriminating or impartial; mutual or unilateral, as necessary.

$$\triangle \heartsuit <$$

☐ If one is completely identified with Christ and his coming in the world then when one dissolves back into the elements of matter, he has lost nothing. All really cared about, the life and growth of Love unto the perfect community will be attained anyway. (I am sort of looking forward to being <u>consciously</u> dissolved and re-entered into nature and eternal Life, body AND soul.)

△♡<

☐ My opinions on some current theological beliefs:

   ☐ 1. People say "God is bisexual or asexual." I say, "God is male, inseminator of the Universe".

   ☐ 2. People say, "God created the world." I say, "God is creating, (by fathering) the world."

   ☐ 3. People say, "God is omnipotent". I say, "God is not all powerful. He is all the Power: LOVE.

   ☐ 4. People say, "God rules". I say, "God overrules".

   ☐ 5. People say, "The Bible is the word of God". I say, "The Bible is a record of the development of human consciousness, and understanding of God and Life.

△♡<

☐ Christian Love must be a deliberate kind of diffusion: Knowing Love, one must strive to extend it to all, because all are really a part of One.

△♡<

☐ As in the rest of life and the construction of the Universe and music, Fibbonic progression is essential to structure by Love: First, the one, then the couple, then their triad, and after that, union progresses only by group cohesion, not within but added to the original structure:1—1—2—3—5—8—13—21—34—55—89—etc. (Look it up in a math book.)

△♡<

☐ The difference between triune Love and bigamy in life the difference between trying to jump along on both feet at once, or dancing and walking in the beautiful rhythm of nature. Triune Love has its timing and distance right.

△♡<

☐ Only a conviction and realization that there is a God who is Love, Order, and the Source of truth can fit people to live in situations alien to their experience at the same time trying to transform society so that it becomes the best possible according to God's purpose, unlimited by any human vision or concocted utopia.

☐ Nothing, no time, no distance between us; the full power of history, physical and cultural flowing through us. All our daily experiences shared in an instant of touch and transference of person, one to the other. The disintegrations (other relationships) all bound up in one bundle of Love, each one finding, its right position. As in all life, the music and dance become structure, until we are One and "individually members of one another" in order and beauty. The withdrawal and return are repeated, physically and spiritually establishing at last an energy pattern of eternal Love and expansion, in total possession of ourselves and each other, until the web of life engulfs the Whole creation and we know as we are known. The candle is transflamed and the Light of billions of years reveals all things. The cohesion of the universe in expansion depends upon the perpetuation of our Love to faith in One Love.

LIST COMPONENTS OF YOUR OWN PERSON

△♡<

☐ The most interesting observation a person can make of nature is that EVERY DANCE OF LIFE becomes structure (see first, atoms, molecules etc.)—Until it all becomes One Structure, totally conscious and perfectly complex!

△♡<

☐ A FIRST LAW: Organization that is imposed from without, by whatever means, is temporary and artificial. Only those organizations which occur from inner affinities are real and eternal. Examples: families, churches, some marriages, and soul-matings. The Church is the One to which all others must eventually adhere. "That which is bound on Earth shall be bound in Heaven".

△♡<

☐ In the construction of Love, our awareness grows from self, to another, to the triad with its opposite poles of attraction and repulsion which activate the armature of life itself!

△♡<

☐ "The chicken is the invention of an egg that wanted eternal life!" We seek to perpetuate variety in our individual identities. The life is not the body but in the genes. "It is the Spirit that gives life, the flesh has no power". -Jesus. God is literally, Love. Soul-mating is the result of that internal power relating totally, one to a whole other, and must include all that went before in all that is. "Where two or three are gathered in my Nature, there am I". (at the center of things.)

△♡<

☐ The dichotomy between good and evil is simply that one cannot move in opposite directions at once. Either we move toward union (individual, social, cosmic) or we are moving toward disintegration. This holds true at every level of life.

People can be sorted into high and low categories by whether they consider sex a bodily function or a creative expression of Love.

95

Q. How can I feel fulfillment and peace of mind when the longing for my soul-mate is so intense?

A. Obey the drawing power of Love, communicate. But Spirit Love is triune and must be inclusive. You are not whole within yourself......so each person must seek the Divine, through all and above all, the Universal, of which Christ is the Personification. Then that soul will not be in darkness or illusion. There is another part of you, lost, and with which you must reunite, that which is Divine in another (and in every other) personality!

△♡<

"Suffering transforms, matures, and instructs. Suffering increases our capacities of Love and understanding. All suffering makes us have something in common with any of those who suffer. It is the power of communion." -Louis Evely. To try to avoid suffering, growth, being, and becoming more, is wrong. Eventually the "Hound of Heaven" brings us all back to the haven of humanity, whole, real. (The best way to stop the hiccups is to try to hiccup between hiccups! The best way to alleviate suffering is to seek to suffer) for the healing of the broken body of Christ. The soul-mate is the third step in the progression of Eternal life - eternal Love, inclusive.

△♡<

WHAT
LOAVES
AND
FISHES DO
YOU
HAVE

Study "Omegabionics," (ultimate Life-study).

△♡<

That Love which is born of the flesh is flesh: that Love which is born of the Spirit is Spirit.

△♡<

Sexual Love is the recognition of, (and relating to), a particular person at the center of our lives: Do not let your name be "Legion".

△♡<

Life is a sorting process - not as though the music was already written and is now being played, but as though the Composer is trying us together in different chords and sequences to see what comes out music! (to be played later). The ultimate arrangement is the result of our development and relationships in this life. As we grow and become who we are, our inner affinities draw us into harmony in triads and chords of great beauty, for eternal life-in-Love.

△♡<

□ Love does funny things to time,
Evidence of power.
It lengthens or it shortens
A week, a day, an hour.
It draws right things together,
A material creation.
And at the top is Consciousness
Of Love itself: Elation
That cancels hours, days, and weeks.
This is the thing that happens
When the Holy Spirit speaks!

△♡<

□ All of our earthy life is CONTAINED in our eternal life; just as all our childhood is CONTAINED in what we become as adults.

△♡<

□ We are always more aware in great union, and more united in great awareness. The ultimate result of life is total consciousness (awareness) and eternal life in Love (union).

△♡<

□ Love, the HAPPENING: "The Spirit blowing where it will....." We CAN prevent it, but we cannot make it happen. It just comes. When and if we prevent its blooming, we die a little.

△♡<

□ It is good to remember when so many are hearing "voices", that "God has now spoken to us by a Son". And he is our one point of union and unification. So we moved toward the Light, away from all dark, disintegrating, and strange voices.

△♡<

□ You lose everything for which you do not give thanks! You lose it just as surely as though someone came and took it away. Its goodness is not present to your consciousness without appreciation and thanksgiving.

△♡<

□ The Church is, in macrocosm, what individual lives must be in microcosm. We must see Christ in someone, a person who draws our Love, or we cannot Love God whom we have not seen—and for some reason this relationship requires previous commitments on a lower level; marriage, nature, which must be included in the total.

In real Love it is necessary to trust God to finish what he has started! There is no other way: trust and obey! Love. The peak of expression is in the realization of unique identities and relationships. According to Jesus, the purpose of life is the "harvest". The harvest of what? The highest and best from life, the soul, the most developed consciousness, in complexity and communion.

☐   The Bible is like a fallen tree in a dense woods. The majestic giant lies still waiting for all the new, green vines and bushes to assimilate it into useful growth for this day.

☐   All Love, no matter how well expressed, is still more potential than actual.

☐   What is the most highly evolved action of Love? It recognizes and preserves identity, and unites units of consciousness.

☐   First step in evangelism: Catch the attention of men with the thought of God. (God is not in all their thoughts"). Do this by presenting a new and valid concept of some facet of His Being. Such as the fact that His Spirit is truly LOVE, in all its forms. That this creation is of Love, by Love and for Love!

☐   Things take time. Some things may take forever. That is no reason to quit.

☐   The way of the law-abiding citizen is broad and easy and most people go that way But "The way of the transgressor is hard". It is narrow and leads to new things. Not many find it. Only those who give Love supremacy over law.

WRITE A PRAYER ABOUT YOUR LOVE

☐   Oh Lord, I come to Thee because I know that you are the Source of all my Love and all my power to Love. I come to Thee to be led in the beautiful dance of eternal life and Love, for guidance in the use of what I am for the joining, by affinity, my soul in the eternal habitation of thy Spirit with my Loves of this life, and for the future that comes in beauty, in power, in freedom and complexity, all conscious.   Amen.

□ The general resurrection is no problem to God! Have you ever seen a movie run in reverse? That is SORT OF what will happen when we reach the end of time, except that it will all be "shown" at once.

△♡<

□ Oh Living God, increase our Love. This seems a ridiculous thing to pray when our capacities are too Limited to fully express the Love we already have! But Love will find a way. One finger cannot hold back the Sea forever.

△♡<

□ A great Love drives one to seek the diffusion of that spirit throughout all the hours and all the experiences of every day. The sublime union extended into a mutual experience of all life, here and hereafter.

△♡<

□ At its best, sexual expression is the result of preexisting affinity of consciousness.

△♡<

□ Consciousness creates complexity. Then the complexity becomes more and more conscious, and so on to total integration in One Conscious Complex. (That is where eternal identity appears).

△♡<

□ Make us so sure of eternal Love and relationship that we become a Light to all people; the renewal of hope for everlasting life-in-Love; Heaven!

△♡<

□ Help me to live every day perfectly, to the very limit of my abilities, because I have so few days left.

△♡<

April is hope-
Only when one
Like the dawn
Enters and heals.
(THOUGH THE BODY FADES AWAY.)

☐ <u>Re-Source and Re-Search</u>

This is a statistical research method for revealing the consensus of spirit or attitude toward God, in the New Testament. Good statistical research uses and evaluates results obtained from random sampling, (which eliminates personal bias and preference). The value of this practice lies in its ability to make the truth about God's relationship to his creation plain and applicable in the present, by liberating the Light from localisms of time and place.

1. Seven verses are selected at random daily, by whatever method, dice, spinner or simply opening at random and placing a finger, (with the eyes closed,) on a spot on a page, which becomes the verse to copy. <u>This is free random selection.</u>

2. Copy or remember the seven verses, meditating upon each as received and <u>all together</u> to acquire an <u>attitude</u>, or a single impression. Evaluate this thought and consider its positive and negative aspects in relation to your own life this day.

Prayer is aided by the traditional hand position (finger tips together). Maybe it closes an energy circuit? Anyway, I find that I cannot put my hands in this position without praying!

△♡<

☐ EVERY SINCERE PRAYER GETS <u>PROCESSED</u>. The process usually involves time.

△♡<

☐ It is a serious and basic mistake to call God or Spirit "she". By doing this we make the Earth and the Universe lesbian! It has no male principle at all! God is One. And this One of course includes the male and female principles, but Jesus was quite specific about calling God, "Father". That is the difference between pantheism and Christianity. We believe in a Person who has impregnated the Earth for its salvation/fulfillment. Because the human mind cannot attain a higher concept, but in attempting to go beyond the Person falls back to a mechanistic thought. The Male includes the female in Essence; the female includes the male in incubation/incarnation!

△♡<

☐ God is inclusive. The wilder and more illogical your belief in a good, Personal God the truer it is! This is the truth that opposes entropy: the impossible Consciousness that creates man, dinosaurs, butterflies, and whales! Imagination and life are truer than logic and entropy. We give God glory when we think of him anthropomorphically. Life overcomes entropy; God overwhelms logic, (although he is also the source of reason (logos) and the fountain of Truth.) He is infinitely conscious and totally complex.

△♡<

☐ I trust you. But I also realize that in giving myself so completely, I subject myself to the possibility of total anhialation! If you should be unfaithful, I would be destroyed. The risk is possible because our primary allegiance, both yours and mine, is to one who cannot be unfaithful, and saves us both through that dedication, in our whole identity. (It is in giving that we receive. -St. Francis)

☐ By the year 2000 the Whole Earth should be as obedient to the Spirit of Love as nature now is to instinct.

△♡<

Awareness. Veined petal.
Stinging nostril, trembling
Muscle. Tears.

△♡<

He who will not fully
Enter the Structure of Love,
Hinders others.

△♡<

☐ Expect, wait for, and grow into eternal Love: perfect union and order outside the limitations of this Earth life. We each have our own place and relationship close or remote, with each and EVERY other.

△♡<

☐ For mind over matter it is mind that matters! We must learn that feeling is just the "tail that wags the dog!" It is not the end that should govern life's direction!

△♡<

☐ The most obvious of all laws active in the life of spirit is that we receive, in multiplied proportion what we give, and have taken away what we withhold.

△♡<

☐ Complaining is the opposite of praise. If praise and Love are the true "end of man", complaining must be travel in the wrong direction!

△♡<

Faith: Trust in God, -
The potential truth of unborn planets
Unlit stars!

△♡<

101

Unless I include all those you love in my Love, I exclude part of you. Unless I include all those God loves in my Love, I exclude part of God.

THE BELL OF FAITH

I let go of every nailed down thing,
To the bell-rope of Thy Love
I cling.
That God Lives, and knows, and cares,
I risk my all. And swing!
Showered by the bell-notes as they fall
And bring - - - -
New Consciousness!
This is the way to know
The bell will ring.

GIVING

Self-will has ached itself to death and found
New self! All free, faith-filled, unbound.
Lingering longings fall
Into place,
I see my trust and Love light up YOUR face!
Heaven here; where every precious thing
Is made of Light,
And every molecule alive
By Spirit's might.
The fear this holy thing would die;
Allowed to be, then pass,
(With all that is you or me)
Overcome at Last!
Because I can believe
God does give Love
And pain relieve.
The only way to Love
Is through self-giving.

No sane person lives long without doubting his own sanity.

PEACE

Peace
is not a thing
To be made.
Peace
And the new age
Must be born.
But the prehistoric
Patterns pregnant time.

The Benefactor
Being
Overcomes.
Overwhelms.
Overgives.

Order
To be trusted
Beyond our minds.
"Do not resist evil!"
(Resisting compounds power)
Uncover its negative nature
In the martyr's
Finishing hour.
Accept.
Receive.
Violence.
Hatred.
Assimilate.
Transmute.
Victory for life!
The ecstacy
And agony
Of Love.
Love.
Inclusive.
Peace.

103

☐ The explanation of the Christian feeling of intense unity in worship is that with our eyes upon God, we stand in the same spot, not successively but simultaneously! The first law of matter is that two things cannot occupy the same space at the same time, but a law of the spirit is that souls can occupy the same "space" at the same time, filled with the same Spirit!

△♡<

☐ Let there be a confluence of the Spirit among those who worship and seek Thee, that this may be another means of consummation.
Person to PERSON call completed: finds creation once repeated!

△♡<

☐ "Man cannot live on bread alone".
(Or on anything else.........alone).
"But on every word of the living God".
HE SPEAKS EVERY LEAF AND STONE!

△♡<

☐ "God is everywhere. If we could see God we couldn't see anything else." (Nathan Shores - age 6 years).

△♡<

☐ "These lilacs are just like people who went to sleep and forgot to wake up." (Melody Shores - age 4). She sensed the unconscious life.

△♡<

☐ We live in a Make/Believe world: Believe and Make.

△♡<

☐ Christians make sexual expression a sacrament of personal Love: The deepest and most holy communion of persons in the Presence of God. Others find it a sort of necessary phenomenon of selfish instinct; a more or less compulsive drive which rapidly loses its capacity to please, or translate feeling into structure. The first, continues to increase in depth an meaning, as it becomes more and more an expression of the All to one. The second, becomes less and less satisfying, and loses all its meaning as it disintegrates in plurality through the fruitless search for sensation (promiscuity), or dies in the selfish convenience of monogamy.

△♡<

☐ **A B C Semantics and Definitions**

CORRECT THESE DEFINITIONS IF NEEDED

A. Adultery.	Substitution of one person for another.
B. Belief.	Conviction. To make use of the will in matters which go beyond reason.
C. Charity.	Self-giving action.
D. Divorce.	Separation of what Love has joined.
E. Evangelism.	Truth telling.
F. Faith.	Trust (requiring action)
G. God.	Love. The Person. Cohesive Power who creates, sustains, and unites all things. LIGHT. SPIRIT.
H. Heaven.	Pattern of perfection.
I. Include.	To add another within One.
J. Jesus.	A man in whom God revealed his Person and purpose.
K. Kingdom.	Wherever <u>One</u> rules.
L. Love.	The power of cohesion, integration, and differentiating union.
M. Man.	(male and female) Organism of the greatest Earthly complexity.
N. Name. Nature.	Identification.
O. Omnipotence.	All power.
P. Providence.	God's present creative activity.
Q. Quote.	Repeat.
R. Redeem.	To provide for debt (lack).
S. Spirit.	Essence.
T. Triad. Triangle. Trinity.	The basic structural units of music, architecture, Love and life. THREE.
U. Understand.	To know with the mind and heart.
V. Vision.	Projected and partially realized hope.
W. Worship.	To be aware of and respond to God.
X. The Cross.	Symbol of self-giving and victorious life:
Y. You.	Identity.
Z. Z.	(Omega) The <u>CON</u>-clusion.

△♡<

☐ To know that one arm cannot be saved without saving the rest of the Body is to provide a great motivation for trying to save the Whole Earth. To know that nothing is saved until all is saved is to catch the real vision of Shalom and the reason for the coming of Christ.

△♡<

☐ God prepared a banquet of Love, and sent out invitations to all kinds of people, but everyone was too "busy" to come.

△♡<

☐ So much of the sentimental, play-acting "Christian" performances are blasphemy! It is like plastering pink stucco all over the Great Stone Face.

△♡<

☐ A duplication of effort is to be encouraged if it will produce a duplication of results!

△♡<

☐ Each person has two poles of relationship: one active, one passive. (one positive and one negative) They are both necessary to the functioning of Love.

△♡<

☐ The Kingdom of God includes Real Love, that specialized, center to center, person to person, affinity which is the highest pinnacle of complex consciousness.

△♡<

☐ God's stated purpose is the salvation of everything: The ideal sequel to the creation of everything.

△♡<

☐ Major task of the future: Complementary relationships in complex personal structures of functioning groups.

△♡<

☐ What does Earth want? More Love in Life.

△♡<

☐ Virtue defined: Feeling, translated into structure, toward the greatest complexity and consciousness.

△♡<

☐ The purpose of life is identity. We live to become who we are, altogether.

△♡<

☐ May the new truth of <u>eternal Love</u> be revealed like a second sun rising at dawn alongside the old sun (<u>eternal life</u>) astounding and inescapable!

△♡<

☐ Whatever else it may be, the Church is becoming the reconstituted Body of Christ.

△♡<

☐ Is a mutual Love a short-circuited Love? Not if the distance between encompasses the Earth.

△♡<

☐ If every person had a soul-mate, in whom he could see God, one with whom he could be in total union and communion as the Spirit provided opportunity so that life flowed on two levels like a great musical composition, how beautiful life could be! What patience and accomplishment; what reverence and dedication. The whole creation could sing in peace. Everyone's utmost concern would be the expression of Love on every level, in gratitude for the fullness of this Love, above and beyond all relationships on the natural level. Much grace and growth would blossom in hard and disciplined hearts, set free. No man would judge his neighbor harshly, but in his own sweet passion would forgive and bless every soul with whom he had to do, living beyond greed and pettiness, brushing off all kinds of persecution or violated rights as of no importance in comparison with the potential of Love in time.

△♡<

☐ This life I now live, I live by faith in God-is-Love, the One Holy Spirit revealed in and through Jesus the Christ, Saviour of the World (and every individual part of it) by drawing all things together in their right order, establishing the structure of eternal Life-in-Love.

△♡<

☐ Structure is simply a dance remembered and repeated. (See atoms and molecules). Eternal life is God's "total recall"!

△♡<

☐ The world's greatest need is to become united. There must be a Center around which it can organize itself. Jesus, the Christ, was sent to be that Center.

△♡<

107

Dance

I step out to dance this day
To dance it to Thy music
To dance the dawn
To dance the noon
To dance the moonlight
I dance the minutes
Dance the hours
Time and rhythm flowing
I dance my Love
I dance my life
I know where I am going!

☐   Freedom is the ability to act from internal motivation as opposed to external coercion, and depends upon complexity and consciousness, to be.

△♡<

☐   Without the eternal triangle there is no POINT to life!△

△♡<

☐   You never lead us into temptation, but always leads us out of the "evil" we are already in, for this is evolution; to draw all things up to Thee.

"Those who live in love have an advantage over others: they know the power of God, and remember what Heaven will be like."

"When I'm not near the [Person] I Love, I Love the [Persons] I'm Near."
-The King and I

To build a cohesive society we must first of all recognize that Wholeness is composed of complexity,- and simplification can only eliminate superfluous details. The heart of the matter is to produce <u>harmony</u> among multitudes of greatly varying parts. Inter-cultural cohesion and the recognition that the purpose of cultures is the development of persons and groups into communicating societies results in greater complexity, greater consciousness, wholeness and oneness: —That is, more and greater culture and higher and more developed human beings in combination with each other.

The principle of cohesion among persons is love. So we must embark upon the application of love to cultural expression: The affinity of persons, and the perfect place for each individual, cannot be found outside the Whole.

Music is a bridge
On which solitudes
May meet.
Music is a fire
That consumes us
With its heat....
Except that rhythm
Is a river flowing -
On our hands and feet!
Music, then, is LOVE
Making time (so briefly) sweet.
Music is a bridge
On which solitaries Meet.

109

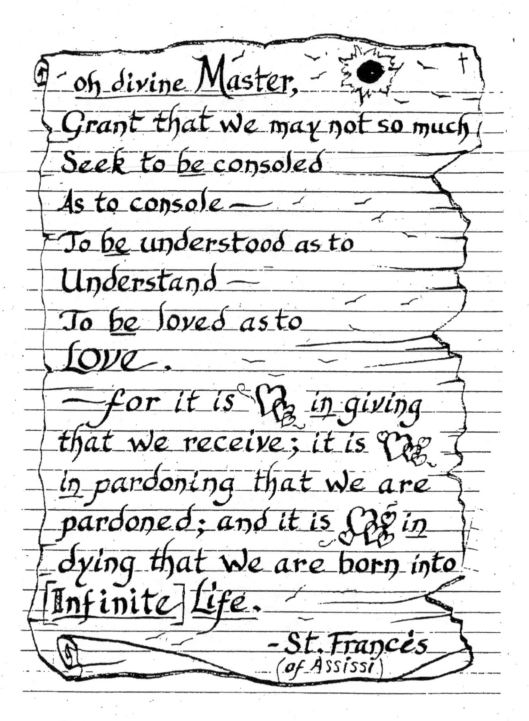

oh divine Master,

Grant that we may not so much

Seek to be consoled

As to console —

To be understood as to

Understand —

To be loved as to

Love.

— for it is 🖤 in giving

that we receive; it is 🖤

in pardoning that we are

pardoned; and it is 🖤 in

dying that we are born into

[Infinite] Life.

— St. Francés
(of Assissi)

It was less than 100 years
from the horse and buggy
to the moon! How soon
will man learn to live in
perfectly synchronized,
complementary activity?
It will be music, love, & God!

God rules and overrules:
every lack of life is
being overcome.
—
Life is a sorting process:
we are arranged by,
our development and
our internal affinities.

The Words of Christ,
Himself: If you remain
in me and my words
remain in you. ask
whatever, you will and it
shall be done for you.—John
See also: John 6:63—15:7

A UNIQUELY HUMAN RESPONSIBILITY

Men still want to have the authority over "their" women that the cavemen had!

I believe that late abortions are wrong, but in the early stages of a pregnancy, abortion may sometimes be the right thing—the lesser of two evils. Spontaneous abortions occur naturally and frequently when there is some abnormality in the fetus or other cause. We should at least allow an induced abortion when the fault that the embryo was not ejected was the poor functioning of the mother's body.

If men can demand that every fertilized egg be brought to term let them consider the waste of billions mandated by nature!

Because women are used to the monthly evacuation of their "premises" and the "waste" of the human egg, they know that higher considerations are more important. An error, discovered early, may legitimately be evaluated in the light of the living, potential and future probabilities of life. I am aware of the human shape of an early fetus, but I also know, and so do you, the blob of protoplasm is not yet a person.

I am opposed to abortion casually on demand such as is implied in the phrase "pro-choice," because I believe that God is concerned about which shall be born, and which shall be aborted. God has purposes, beyond the physical, that demand our prayerful obedience. If a fertilized egg developing in a women, under certain circumstances, is not according to the Will of God, a spiritual and moral decision must be made.

Anyone who believes in God's creative power can realize that a physically defective embryo may still have great potential and should be brought to full term. But another, also of God's guidance, might need to be aborted before it becomes a person. These are spiritual mysteries. Human beings share both the creation and the responsibility for the whole and interdependent relationships of life.

Each pregnancy should be conceived only by the will of God. When it is not, further guidance is needed to discover what God wills in each specific situation. Abortion is a religious issue and cannot be dictated or prohibited by the government, or any other external authority.

IF A MISTAKE HAS BEEN MADE IT SHOULD BE CORRECTED:

As a person lies dying, artificial support systems are removed when the brain ceases to function. A fetus is not a person until the brain begins to co-ordinate the body (about the third month.)

Light has a Source.

Darkness has no source, but is everywhere not yet filled by the Light.

"Through our thoughts and our human experiences, we long ago became aware of the strange properties which make the universe so like our flesh:

like the flesh it attracts us by the charm which lies in the mystery of its curves and folds, and in the depths of its eyes;

like the flesh, it disintegrates and eludes us when submitted to our analysis..............

as with the flesh, it can only be embraced in the endless reaching out to attain what lies beyond the confines of what has been given to us.

Once upon a time men took into your temple the first fruits of their harvests, the flower of their flocks. But the offering, you really want...........is nothing less than the growth, of the world borne ever onward in the steam of universal becoming."

ABOVE QUOTES FROM—Teilhard De Chardin

113

A Theory—

After God's Thesis (Word), there is the antithesis,— Then God's synthesis. —M.S.

............and this I am sure of............. a desire, irresistable, hollowing, which makes us cry out, believer and unbeliever alike: 'Lord, make us One.'

.............it is the Light, existing before all else was made which, patiently, surely eliminates our darkness.

.............It is a terrifying thing to have been born...................

—Teilhard de Chardin

—HYMN OF THE UNIVERSE - P. 99

In Christ we share—

1. The happiness of personal growth,
2. The happiness of eternal union, —body, and soul,
3. The happiness of endless LOVE and identification with all nature, all creation, all that is and all that is to be — unlimited and eternal Life.

—TEILHARD

EPH. 1:9+10

114

Holy One, Being, Spirit, Love and Life; fill the human race, in all its variety, with your Truth and Beauty, that all people may supplement each other, One world in functioning wholesomeness.

For the fulfillment of your purpose, use us who feebly and fiercely try to do thy will, in all its unfathomable mystery!

Let the tide of LOVE swiftly rise until all life is swept along in the Sea of its fulness. Let every child, from birth, recognize and embrace you in all things, until they all become one in you, varied parts of the great conscious-complexity.

THROUGH JESUS WHO WAS SENT TO SAVE THE WORLD BY LOVE AND TRUTH - FOR LOVE, AND IN Love FOREVER.

The Followship

Love God with all your heart;

—AND THERE SHOULD BE AT LEAST TWELVE PEOPLE WITH WHOM YOU MAINTAIN CONTINUOUS COMMUNION. (SEE JESUS).

FORM A FOLLOWSHIP GROUP

Love God with all your soul;

—HEAR THE TEACHINGS OF JESUS, (DAILY) FOR INSPIRATION, ATTITUDE AND DIRECTION. HEAR, TO A LESSER EXTENT, THE REST OF THE BIBLE (DISCRIMINATING BETWEEN MYTH AND HISTORY). PRAY. "ALWAYS, AND FOR EVERYTHING, GIVE THANKS."

Love God with all your mind;

—HAVE REVERENCE FOR ALL TRUTH, AND USE IT TO PRODUCE PERFECTION AND FULFILLMENT FOR ALL. SPEAK TO GOD VERBALLY, (IN NON-ORAL SPEECH OR WRITING).

Love God with all your strength;

—LET LOVE BE INCLUSIVE — AND CONTROLLED: STRUCTURED BY THE HOLY SPIRIT. VISUALIZE AND FACILITATE THE COMING OF SHALOM: GO AND DO.

Love your neighbor as yourself.

—MAINTAIN RELATIONS:
  I. NATURAL - (MARRIAGE AND FAMILY)
  II. SPIRITUAL - (SOUL-MATES AND FRIENDS)
  III. VOLCATIONAL - (THOSE CALLED TOGETHER TO WORK FOR THE FULFILLMENT OF GOD'S PURPOSES.)
  IV. DO UNTO ALL JUST WHAT YOU WANT TO DO. THEM

God is One. God is Spirit. God is Love: Light.

— UNITING — UNIFYING — UNIVERSING —

Whatever Is Better Will Be." — Teilhard

THE LIGHT SHINES IN THE DARK; AND DARKNESS CANNOT PUT IT OUT. — JOHN I

D.C

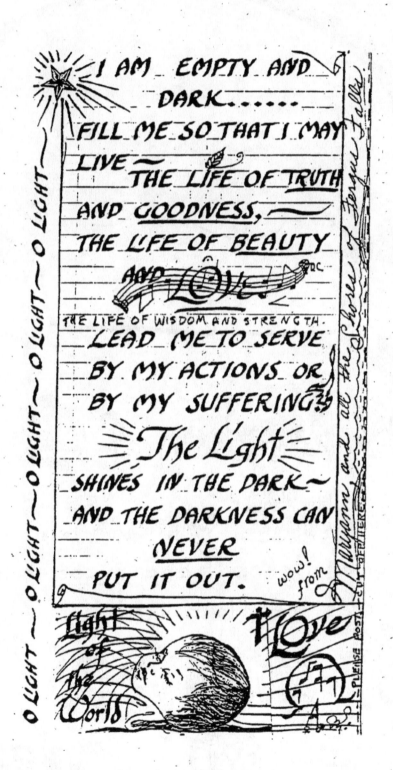

(PART OF A PRAYER BY THE BISHOP OF BLOMFONTAINE)

117

"The Kingdom of God is like yeast..... A woman takes it and mixes it in six measures of flour until................. it all rises" - Jesus

Make the whole Earth rise
to new balance and beauty,
With the fire of inclusive Love.

One Earth, - one humanity; "to be

or not to be, that is the question."

SOME OF THE TRUTH ABOUT LOVE

A COLORING BOOK

Lucie + M. Shores

OUR GOAL IS SPIRITUAL UNION SO COMPLETE THAT PHYSICAL UNION BECOMES, FIRST, INCIDENTAL AND FINALLY UNNECESSARY. LOVE IS THE MEANS OF UNION.

REAL, SUFFERING, LOVE FORCES PRAYER. IT IS A SPIRITUAL PROCESS NOT TO BE GROUNDED IN THE FLESH.

THE ATTEMPT TO EXPRESS LOVE BY PURELY BIOLOGICAL MEANS RESULTS IN DEEP DEPRESSION, BECAUSE OF THE REALIZATION OF THE LIMITATIONS OF THE BODY IN TIME AND SPACE. LOVE IS ETERNAL.

LOVE MUST BE CONTROLLED, REPLACING THE CHAOS IN HUMAN EVENTS WITH THE BEAUTIFUL TIMING AND ORDER OF THE GALAXIES.

DO NOT STIR A LIVE VOLCANO WITH A DEAD STICK.

IT IS ONLY AN ACTUAL RELATIONSHIP TO GOD THAT SUSTAIN LOVE AND, THEREFORE, EVENTUALL PEACE. THERE IS NO OTHER SOURCE OF LOVE

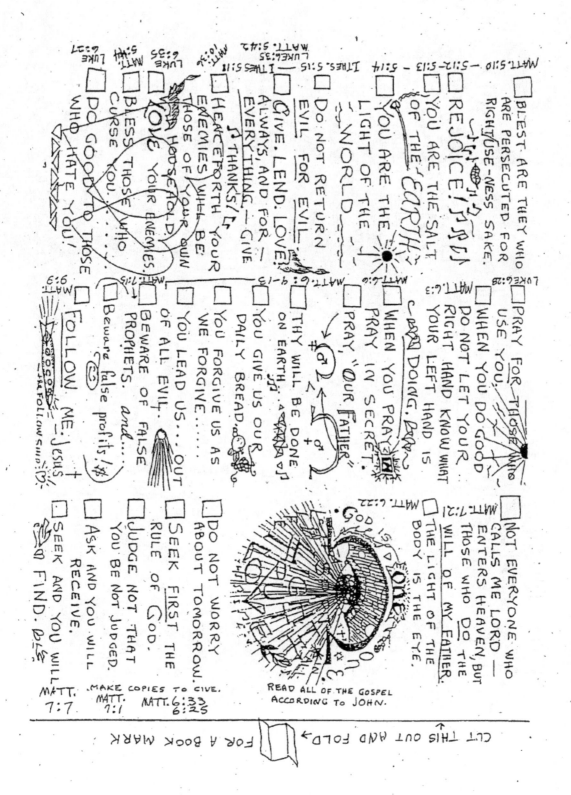

BLEST ARE THEY WHO ARE PERSECUTED FOR RIGHTeouS-NESS SAKE. MATT. 5:10

REJOICE!♪♪♪ — 5:12 — MATT. 5:11

YOU ARE THE SALT OF THE EARTH!

YOU ARE THE LIGHT OF THE WORLD. MATT. 5:13 — 5:14

Do NOT RETURN EVIL FOR EVIL. 1THES 5:15

GIVE. LEND. LOVE! ALWAYS, AND FOR EVERYTHING. — GIVE THANKS! LUKE 6:35

HENCEFORTH YOUR ENEMIES WILL BE THOSE OF YOUR OWN HOUSEHOLD. MATT. 10:36

LOVE YOUR ENEMIES. LUKE 6:35

BLESS THOSE WHO CURSE YOU. MATT. 5:44

DO GOOD TO THOSE WHO HATE YOU! LUKE 6:27

PRAY FOR THOSE WHO USE YOU. LUKE 6:28

WHEN YOU DO GOOD, DO NOT LET YOUR RIGHT HAND KNOW WHAT YOUR LEFT HAND IS DOING. MATT. 6:3

WHEN YOU PRAY PRAY IN SECRET. PRAY, "OUR FATHER" MATT. 6:6

THY WILL BE DONE ON EARTH... MATT. 6:9-13

YOU GIVE US OUR DAILY BREAD.

YOU FORGIVE US AS WE FORGIVE......

YOU LEAD US...OUT OF ALL EVIL.

BEWARE OF FALSE PROPHETS. and..... MATT. 7:15
Beware false profits!

FOLLOW. ME.-Jesus MARK 9:9
Follow ship...

NOT EVERYONE WHO CALLS ME LORD — ENTERS HEAVEN, BUT THOSE WHO DO THE WILL OF MY FATHER. MATT. 7:21

THE LIGHT OF THE BODY IS THE EYE. MATT. 6:22

God is ONE

READ ALL OF THE GOSPEL ACCORDING TO JOHN.

DO NOT WORRY ABOUT TOMORROW.

SEEK FIRST THE RULE OF GOD. MATT. 6:33

JUDGE NOT THAT YOU BE NOT JUDGED. MATT. 7:1

Ask AND YOU WILL RECEIVE.

SEEK AND YOU WILL FIND. MATT. 7:7

MAKE COPIES TO GIVE.

CUT THIS OUT AND FOLD → FOR A BOOK MARK

Happiness is... LOVE?

☐ PEOPLE DO NOT LIVE BY BREAD ALONE, BUT BY EVERY WORD OF GOD. — MATT. 4:4

☐ RIGHTLY DIVIDING IT. *TRUTH* II TIM. 2:15

☐ I HAVE COME AS LIGHT INTO THE WORLD. — Jesus — John 8:12

☐ BLEST ARE THE POOR, (IN SPIRIT). MAT 5 — 5:3 — MATT 5:3

☐ BLEST ARE THEY THAT MOURN (CARE). LUKE 6* — 5:4 — MATT 5:4

☐ BLEST ARE THE MEEK... — 5:5 — MATT 5:5

☐ BLEST ARE THOSE WHO HUNGER AND THIRST FOR RIGHT- USE-NESS... — 5:6 — MATT 5:6

☐ BLEST ARE THE MERCI-FUL. — 5:7 — MATT 5:7

☐ BLEST ARE THE PURE IN HEART... — 5:8 — MATT 5:8

☐ BLEST ARE THE PEACEMAKERS. — 5:9 — MATT 5:9

1.

☐ IF I AM LIFTED UP FROM THE EARTH, I WILL DRAW ALL HU-MANITY TO ME. — Jesus John 12:32

☐ BELIEVE IN THE LIGHT... THAT YOU MAY BE CHILDREN OF LIGHT. John 12:36

☐ I KNOW THAT THE FATHER'S COMMAND ORDER IS LIFE EVERLASTING. John 12:50

☐ FEAR NOT. THERE IS NOTHING HIDDEN THAT SHALL NOT BE REVEALED...THAT SHALL NOT BE KNOWN. LUKE 8:17
LUKE 8:11

☐ A NEW COMMAND I GIVE YOU LOVE EACH OTHER! — E=MC² — It IS THE SPIRIT THAT GIVES LIFE,... THE WORDS I HAVE SPOKEN ARE SPIRIT AND LIFE. — Jesus John 13:34   John 6:63
6.

☐ DO TO OTHERS WHAT YOU WANT DONE TO YOU.

☐ I WANT MERCY, NOT SACRIFICE.

☐ ONE WHO LOSES HIS LIFE FOR MY SAKE WILL FIND IT! Jesus

☐ FOR GOD SO LOVED THE WORLD THAT HE SENT HIS ONLY SON THAT WHOEVER BE-LIEVES IN HIM SHALL NOT DIE BUT SHALL HAVE ETERNAL LIFE.

☐ FOR GOD DID NOT SEND HIS SON INTO THE WORLD TO CON-DEMN THE WORLD, BUT THAT THE WORLD MIGHT BE SAVED THROUGH HIM.

☐ PUT NEW WINE INTO NEW SKINS AND BOTH WILL BE SAVED.

MATT. 7-12   MATT. 9:13   MATT. 10:39   John 3:16   John 3:17   MATT. 9:11

5.

128

CHOOSE THIS DAY

CHECK
BOXES
DAILY

the SAVIOR   or   DESTROYER

MATTHEW 19:26

John 3:17 + Eph. 1:10

Eph. 4:15+16 LUKE 4:18+19

☐ Life

☐ Co-operation

☐ progression

☐ Trust

☐ Forgiveness

☐ Truth

☐ Knowledge

☐ Praise

☐ Unity

☐ LOVE (inclusive)

=s More "Being

in greater Union."

—TEILHARD

PEACE

One above, through and in all.

REVELATION 9:7-11

Revelation: John's visions/alternative.

☐ Death

☐ Conflict

☐ regression

☐ Suspicion

☐ Condemnation

☐ Untruth

☐ Ignorance

☐ Complaining

☐ Division

☐ HATE (of any)

=s Less Being;

disintegration/death.

CHAOS

THERE has been set before us a high
way and a low, and it is for us to
choose the way the world will
go.

Maryann Shores
Fegus Falls, Route 3

129

"There is one God, and Earth is His prophet. The beauty of things is the face of God: Worship it. Give your Hearts to it; labor to be like it." -Jeffers

There is one God, and the Earth is his Love. The "Beauty of things is God's face". (Seek his reflection in the still pond and beyond the tree top's green lace.) Seek and follow the Truth of his Son, Who was planted and born of the Earth. In seeking you'll find the Center and Mind and be brought to your own second birth. For Jesus re-entered the Earth, when he died. As he said, he is always among us. Truth, encrusted with falsehoods and pride must be born anew, (and from us). the Earth is the pregnant Mother, to give children their Father's face. His beauty is found in the sights and sounds of all life, and the human race. So we slough off the mold and slime of ages (some is as old as writing), to open our hearts to Earth's delights. Our eyes were made for lighting! There is one God, and Earth grows his Word. (He speaks every leaf and stone). So while she lives the Earth is our hope God's Seed within her sown.

THE MYSTERY:
WE'RE IN JESUS, "THE WAY–THE TRUTH–AND THE LIFE"–HERE, AND HEREAFTER.–SO BE IT.
HE IN US

Quotes from L. James Koch-(as he understands me)

☐ What can we do to support family life; marriage, as an institution?

△♡<

☐ What can we do to help fulfill the human potential of each person, and all people together?

△♡<

☐ What can we do to increase the joy of living throughout a lifetime; the joy that is found in Love being expressed?

△♡<

☐ What can we do to build positive peace; the harmony triune? A triadic social structure as opposed to the dyadic polarization that is destroying the world?

△♡<

☐ The Eternal Triangle is the emotional equivalent of war, given to us to build with, through the Soul-Mating phenomenon.

△♡<

☐ This book Triune Love THE ETERNAL TRIANGLE REVISITED, attempts to reveal a kind of Love which includes, but transcends, brotherly, and the erotic forms of Love which currently dominate our Western culture. THE SPIRITUAL DIMENSION OF LOVE WHICH INCLUDES GOD IN LOVE–MAKING, IS NECESSARY FOR SOUL-MATING.

△♡<

☐ But soul-mating, with its requirements of integrity, empathy, and risk, is not readily grasped or accepted, emotionally.

△♡<

✡

MARK
T - F
OR
MAYBE

☐ When we think of inter personal relationship with any degree of intimacy an cohesiveness, we too often equate it with marriage relationship; the natural, human convention produced for the purpose of integrating persons, physically, into nuclear family units, for the support and growth of all its members.

131

☐ Too often the emotional projection of the idea of marriage onto a different relationship does not allow for the development of a higher level of interpersonal intimacy.

△♡<

☐ Marriage is a specific relationship of specific persons for the purpose of building a family of two or more. The partners do actually become one flesh.

△♡<

☐ Soul-mating is a <u>different</u> relationship of specific persons interacting in spiritual communion to build with God, through LOVE, the <u>universe</u>. In so doing they also become One.

△♡<

☐ A couple can be happily married while the individuals relate to other persons at many different levels. Social structure as truly as structure of matter in general is as dance remembered and repeated. (This table is an atomic square dance)!

△♡<

☐ What can we do then to improve the quality of our living as persons constantly, dynamically involved with each other at all levels of human experience?

△♡<

☐ If we consider soul-mating a more integrative and inclusive form of human behavior we must, first, look at structure as we find it everywhere. And as Buckminster Fuller, creator of the geodesic sphere, has pointed out "Triangle <u>IS</u> structure." The triad, triangle, and even the trinity remind us of this fact.

△♡<

☐ Not to rewrite what is found in the book, but to emphasize its practical application, individual "needs and feelings are included in <u>more</u> that <u>one</u> other person's needs and feelings.

△♡<

☐ The tensegrity complex is essential. Just as the geodesic dome structure is one of the strongest in architecture, so is the triadic, inter-personal, human support system. There is a dynamic, supportive interaction always going on between persons in this complex social-spiritual structure.

△♡<

☐   Soul-mating does not allow promiscuous or irresponsible love-making. Soul-mating supports and is dependent upon good natural marriage: Soul-mating cannot occur where divorce or separation have destroyed the base of the triangle.

☐   Marriage does not allow soul-mating <u>within</u> the marriage; marriage <u>is</u> included <u>within</u> the wholeness of the soul-mating, (and other affinities).

☐   Soul-mating is completely outside the marriage, thus keeping the marriage intact at the center of the persons' lives.

☐   Soul-mating is a complex, inclusive concept of responsible Love behavior and Love relationship initiated by, and never cut off, from, the Spirit of holiness, and the Living One, God.

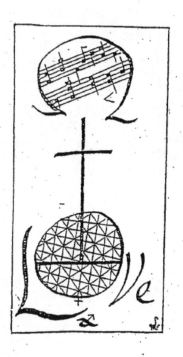

"Real Love moves: from the disire for the greatest pleasure with the least effort, to the desire for total, sacrificial, self-giving effort."
— Teilhard

— *for the beloved One.*
— M. Shores

133

Debatable Questions

Answers to questions:

a. Marriage results in a kind of osmosis until the two persons become one unit. When this is achieved the individuals who are now, normally, not attracted to each other, mistakenly think that they should try to repeat (experience) the <u>process</u>, or separate!

b. What is needed, of course, is new "solution" added to one or the other to unbalance the dead level. This is the motivating energy of structure in human life. The process is intrinsic to the triune structure of microcosm and macrocosm, alike. The soul-mates find/create one another as part of God's activity in the on-going complexification of human life. Awareness grows with gravitation toward Omega. A sorting process is necessary for structure. <u>Right people to the right people at the right time!</u>

c. The mystics who teach "unity with Self alone" have not recognized what Teilhard found, that "union differentiates". That is, there is a structure. There are components of the Self. And, as Buckminster Fuller pointed out, all "structure is triangle". Teilhard carefully pointed out the difference between: spiritual regression, (returning to the uncreated, Substance-Self Eastern religions), and progression, toward the Total-Self, Complexity-consciousness (Western religion) concepts of Union.

See: THE NEW MYSTICISM -by Ursula King

P.S. Science has also recently shown that below the quark are particles which exist only in triplicate!

TRIUNE PEACEMAKING

SUSPEND THE PAST. FOCUS ON THE
FUTURE. DIVIDE GROUPS INTO THREES;
DETERMINE INDIVIDUALS' GOALS.
FORMULATE AN <u>ULTIMATE GOAL</u>.
INTEGRATE-FACILITATE: UNITY.

FORM
AN
AFFINITY
GROUP

Jesus said, "Where two or three are gathered in my [nature] there I Am." He was speaking for God in himself.

In order to actually realize the Love of God we must attain the emotional level of what would be infatuation if it were focused upon one person but which, when balanced by two or three, transcends human limitations and makes God real to us. We must Love persons deeply to be able to Love God, the unseen, as He is.

Because of the two main facets (left and right) of every person, each one requires, at least two or three certain individuals in a permanent relationship, in order to be a whole being, and to solidify the whole social structure in unity, fulfillment and peace. (Lesser facets require lesser relationships.)

When this deep level of inclusive, identifying Love is reached, Love for all others and the Whole Universe blossoms! All relationships are deepened; humanity is linked and cemented together for the elimination of all feelings of hatred, alienation and separation. An uncollapsable interior structure is formed in triadic union, the tetrahedron of geodisic spheres.

Triune (and scheduled) Love is the next step to peace on Earth. The One God is recognized in and through, and transcending all. A new age of Love and peace is born! The secrets of Christ, so long misunderstood and perverted by human customs and tradition, will stand revealed. Love requires structure and timing, like music.

NOTES:

O Holy Spirit of God, as I lie down to sleep I know that my mind returns to Your great Mind/Love. In my sleep and dreaming your Light penetrates and corrects my life. You fill and ernergize me that I may live your Love, (to the whole Earth in all its parts).

When I awake from finished sleep, having read from your Word, I carry within new power and Light to think and do what I want thought and done to me, uniting all life in functioning elegance.

In returuning and in rest you shall be saved.

— Isaiah 30:15

— M. Shores

When a union of human beings is both physically & spiritually consummated it needs to be maintained, and another begun! Continuously more and higher consciousness is produced only by progressively uniting it in greater and greater complexity of order, by inclusively structuring and scheduling Love.

SHOULD
LOVE
BE
FELT?

SPIRITUAL RELATIONSHIP, and
the INNER AFFINITIES that come
with sharing truth and beauty,
are as essential to truly human
life as food and drink.
To limit depth and intense
expression of *LOVE* to a single
relationship, such as marriage,
is to commit an unforgivable sin
against the Spirit. It is time to learn
scheduled, God-guided, and
<u>inclusive</u> *LOVE*, faithful to
each and dedicated to complex
fulfillment for ALL.

—M. Shores

We must realize that we have not yet been born from God's Universe, (inseminated by his light) but have a long way to go before we are <u>perfectly</u> <u>integrated</u> <u>parts</u> of <u>One</u> whole.

We, (and God) are presently manifesting as male or female. God (male) relates to the Universe (female) until he becomes "All in all", and the polarities are perfectly and permanently mated in an unimaginable consummation: the "End of the world"—. Or is it to be "World without end"? Or both. In any case, God is the living Sire producing the Force necessary to complete us (and the Universe). He does not create with is <u>hands</u> but by insemination. "Christ <u>in</u> <u>Us</u>, our hope of glory."

NOT IF. (But When)
-Matt. 7:21-27

When the rains come, and the cave-ins,
And the swirling, rising flood,
And familiar things are dark and strange
In an endless sea of mud,
We better have a house of years
On the rock of obedience silled.
When the pounding tides of life come in,
It is too late to build.

139

Summary

by
MARYANN
SHORES

●VISION FOR A FUTURE, A PAPER PRESENTED AT THE UNI-
VERSITY FOR PEACE, AT THE UNITED NATIONS IN NEW YORK
CITY, SEPT. 20, 1983, AND PRINTED IN THE BOOK, HUMANI-
TY'S QUEST FOR UNITY, ZONNEVELD (PUB. MIRANANDA,
HOLLAND) AS "A POSITIVE APPROACH TO ACCEPTABLE
PEACE, THE RIGHT USE OF HUMAN ENERGY."

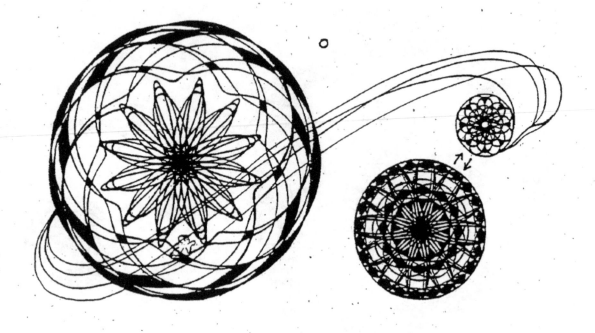

People everywhere are rising up against the terrible threat of nuclear war, but their protests have not brought peace. Humanity needs a new world view.

I will try to present some ideas, based on Teilhard's thought, as a positive approach to peace. My title also speaks of acceptable peace. By this I simply mean a dynamic state of universal good will and fulfillment that most people will not reject; but receive as an ultimate good, in opposition to their present preference for violence as a means of getting what they think they want. I will try to show how freedom, justice, and fulfillment can be brought about without violence, and that peace can be more productive, more vital, and more satisfying than conflict. Real peace is a positive state of harmony and growth. This may be brought about by the right use of human energy. As Teilhard has said: 'Love is the free, creative out-pouring of energy over all unexplored paths.'

Teilhard de Chardin, the French Jesuit priest and paleontologist, set sparks of fire in the dark forest of social chaos. We see them blinking like fire flies in the distance, but upon approaching them we find true light and warmth spreading from his words wherever they are seriously studied and communicated. As the recent publication of the International Teilhard Compendium, *The Desire To Be Human*, shows, his thought inspires persons of many countries all over the world.

Our hope is in this common vision of the Earth being fulfilled to benefit each person, all people, and the whole Earth together.

First of all I want to submit the following pledge of allegiance to the Earth, to include but go beyond loyalty to race or nation.

> *I pledge allegiance to the Earth,*
> *one planet indivisible,*
> *and to the universe in which she lives,*
> *one system under God*
> *with freedom and fulfillment*
> *for the highest life*
> *and consciousness of all.*

The problem of achieving peace begins where it has always been said to begin, in the conflicts within each individual person. What is now being realized is that no individual is or can be whole and complete in himself. In fact no living thing is independent of anything else that exists. And all hang from that which is incomprehensible to humans: Mind alone, provides the cohesive power called Love, the energy holding everything together and builds (against entropy) information that continuously creates greater complexity and consciousness, Everything is good and nothing is perfect.

Nothing has ever been perfect, for perfection implies completeness and nothing is yet completed. I sometimes think of the world as a living, breeding, growing, multiplying jig-saw puzzle!

We must acknowledge that truth, information, understanding, is the way to follow for humanity. (This should include the ineffable light sometimes called enlightenment, which is specific but undefinable).

The Spirit of Truth is the source of Love, whether it is biological (as in sexual attraction), intellectual (as in scientific discovery), aesthetic (as in art), or religious (the attraction, action, awareness of, and interaction with, the One above all, through all and in all). Truth unites those who see it. Truth, bringing Love, is the way to peace. The development and expression of truth in Love is our principal duty. This is the right use of human energy. How, then, should this be?

A NEW SOCIAL STRUCTURE IS REQUIRED FOR THE FUNCTIONING OF LOVE IN THE EARTH.

Imagine a geodesic sphere constructed of triangles held in tensegrity. Structure is triangle, as Buckminster Fuller has pointed out. It is obvious in geometry, music, physics, and architecture. The Trinity, in religions is also an expression of this phenomenon. So we begin to build the Earth using both the natural and spiritual facts of life.

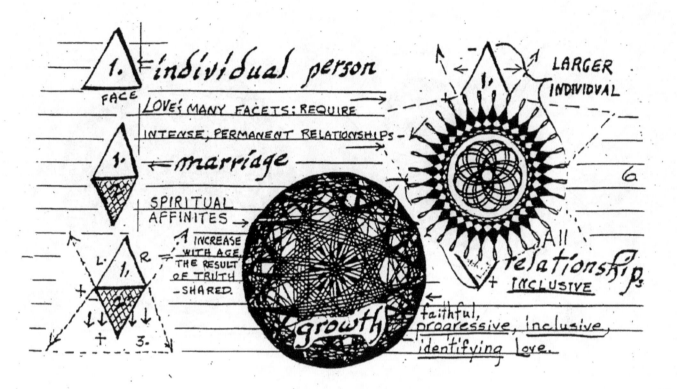

According to Teilhard, Love, the cohesive power that draws and holds things together, existed even when the universe was only made up of random particles. Love brings right things together at the right time, creating first matter, then life, then thought and soul. From pure energy, electrons, protons, neutrons etc., molecules are formed. Molecules brought together in complex combinations have life. Some living structures come together in specialized organization to become conscious. Consciousness in Love has soul.

In the process of development, Love and spiritual affinity also grow. Along with biological evolution, relationships among people developed, including family and tribal structures. Beyond these biological, traditional, or convenient relationships humanity now seeks groupings by intellectual and spiritual affinity, a higher quality of life.

It is generally accepted that some of our goals should be: to get the right food to the hungry at the right time; to get the right information to the right people at the right time. <u>We must now begin to get the right people to the right people at the right time. This is required by Love. As with yeast in making bread, 'She mixes it until it all rises.'</u>

The world is ripe for a social evolution (aided by electronic technology) which bypasses governments, and flows beneath and around the political encumbrances that so pervert human activity.

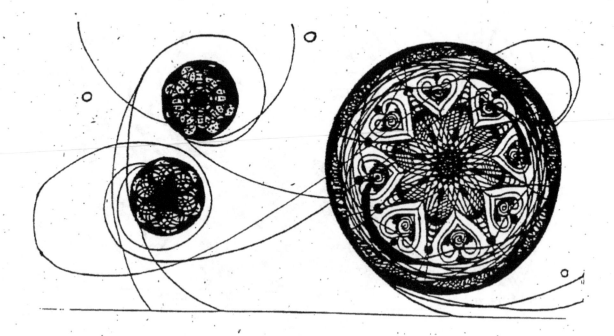

Triune Love, the reunited Eros, Filia, and Agape, which the ancient Greeks had separated, produces integrated individuals, families, and spiritual affinities. It is the theme of most literature, music and art, and holds the possibility of great structural strength for social stability and peace when rightly understood, accepted and used. Repressed and untamed it causes disintegration and destruction by breaking out in uncontrolled violence, the raw power of loose life.

SOCIETY IS BEGINNING TO UNDERSTAND THE NECESSITY FOR SPE-CIALIZATION, FOR INTEGRATING THE GREAT COMPLEXITY, (HUMAN SOCIETY ON EARTH). THIS IS ESPECIALLY DIFFICULT IN THE SUPPLE-MENTAL SPECIALIZATIONS OF INNER AFFINITY, WHICH IS WHERE THE ACTION IS.

Progressive and inclusive love is a controlled Love, replacing the chaos in human events with timing and order.

A glimpse of Love comes to everyone sometime. But people feel that they are deceived by Love's promise. They are driven to despair, violence, escape or materialism subconsciously attempting to find some other way to personal fulfillment which they no longer believe can be found in Love.

146

People need to understand the dimensions of life in Love. The attempts to freeze it, localize it, repress it, express it on only a physical level, or to sublimate it out of existence, all result in despair; for Love forces both the realization of the limitations of the human body, and its capacities. Real, suffering Love is a process not to be grounded in the flesh.

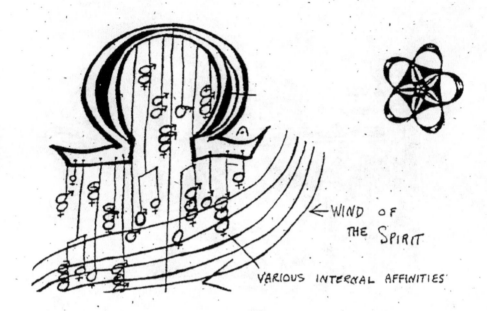

← WIND OF THE SPIRIT

VARIOUS INTERNAL AFFINITIES

We must proceed to spiritual expression, inclusive of, but surpassing, the physical limitations of time and space.

As Teilhard has said: 'Someday, after we have mastered the winds, the waves, the tides, and gravity, we will harness for God the energies of Love: and then for the second time in the history of the world, man will have discovered fire.'

Therefore we can base our hope for a common vision of peace and fulfillment on the beginnings of understanding among people, because Love has been given and needs only to be developed into a structure for the peaceful functioning of humanity in the universe. The way has been provided; it is for us to live it.

WHEN WE LOOK BACK UPON THE DEVELOPMENTS OF THE PAST 100 YEARS, AND SEE HOW HUMANITY HAS GONE FROM THE HORSE AND CARRIAGE TO THE MOON, WE FIND IT POSSIBLE TO BELIEVE IN PEACE WITHIN THE NEXT 100 YEARS!

First of all we must get rid of our fears caused by the notion of separate ownership of separated units by separated units. We are all members of one body; the ear does not own the nose any more then the hand owns the eye. All parts function together at certain times in certain places determined by the Mind and Body as a whole.

147

Second we must get rid of the human obsession with sex. Just because we are not seasonal creatures we need to be shown that this gift has other uses and is only a small part of the great reality permeating everything. It is a power always striving for greater awareness of the great union.

An obsession with sex short circuits the power of Love, a power that must be expressed fully in every way for the perfection of the Earth. We are created to function in an Idea too great for human comprehension; we must strive to meet the challenge.

In understanding that our conflicts come from our own incompleteness, Love gives us a hint of what being complete is like. We are allowed to know, briefly, the ecstacy of union.

In *Science and Christ* Teilhard says, 'fragments that are seeking unity, not a world that is disintegrating. A crisis of birth,* and not symptoms of death. Essential affinities...that is what we are witnessing.' 'When passion is most lofty and noble, the man and woman who come together meet only at the term of their spiritual growth. This law of human union is the law of our cosmic union. Christ holds us by the most material fibers of nature. Nevertheless we shall possess him perfectly only when our personal being and the whole world with it have reached the full limit of their unification.'
'The unification that is being developed so intensively in our time in the human spirit and the human collectivity is the authentic continuation of the biological process that produced the human brain. That is what creative union means.'

* Matt. 24:3-8

148

The ancient religions correctly diagnosed that wars and fightings come from the wars within the individual: one's lust which seems impossible to satisfy, our voracious consuming of everything we get. This intensive drive was placed in us for a purpose: that of building and holding the world together.

The drawing power of this great basic urge is intended for use. As Teilhard states in another place, 'The two come together not for sexual reproduction but to create a world.' Genuine Love, fulfilling a facet of personality otherwise left to disintegrate, must be inclusive, on the way to total unification.

There is the shattering danger of promiscuity which destroys both individuals and the world's hope. This must be overcome by building the structure which Mind and Love require. Nothing can be built on the shifting sands of casual relationships. Truth and Love must draw and hold the right persons together, Overcoming all the disunity and insufficiency on Earth. Peace depends upon this fulfillment. No amount of repression of the primal force can bring peace, but only the awareness of wholeness above all, through all and in all, drawing us together at the right time in right ways, and right places.

Substitution is adultery. Substitution of a person by things, or drugs, or power, or work, or another person, is adultery. Inclusive Love seeks the right place within the whole for each and every part. The whole Earth belongs to everyone and everyone belongs to the Earth.

The structure of life depends upon regularity and scheduling. Our interdependence for maximizing our potential should be structured in time, just as the natural processes of the Earth are structured. This wholeness depends upon the development of individuals, families, other traditional relationships, and spiritual affinities. They are the component parts which produce the new ideas, discoveries, and new life the world needs.

In spiritual affinity there are degrees of instant communion, pre-existent union, the realization and recognition that comes from being already One. When we look into the eyes of someone, openly, in whom this spirit Lives, we know it. Our mutual goal is to function together in truth and Love for the completion of the world.

Involuntary and semi-voluntary relationships, determined by external causes, events, conventions and convenience, are being supplemented by more voluntary associations which are the result of internal affinities.

We are made of our relationships which are expressed in an infinite variety of ways. How conscious we become of the fact that Love requires a body!

A great Love requires all of time and more Being.
There is no way for two to be One, whole,
Until the All, in union, makes One Soul.

The temporary consummations we achieve are to lead us on to the unification of the whole Earth for its final elegance. Or as Teilhard says it is '...the growth of the world, born ever onward in the stream of universal becoming.'

There is One Center of all things. Teilhard calls it 'One point of total consistence.' As a Christian, I call this Center God, the Mind above and within all; and believe, with John, that 'God did not

send his Son into the world to condemn the world, but that the world might be saved through him,' 'For he has made known to us in all wisdom and insight the mystery of his will, according to his purpose which he set forth in christ as a plan for the fullness of time, to unite all things in him - things in heaven and things on Earth.'

Triune Love, progressive and inclusive, is beyond anything we can yet comprehend of glory and beauty, harmony and interaction. These integrities, necessary to the coming of peace, are above and beyond 'good will to all' and conventional family and community relationships, although these are, of course, included. 'The very thing that man did not think could happen is what God has prepared for those who Love him': The Mind of the universe intends that Love shall replace conflict, greed, hatred and separation but it is only by an actual relationship to God that Love is sustained and can eventually bring the peace we dimly perceive. There is no other source of Love.

We must not stir the live volcano of Love with the dead stick of a simple answer.

The truth and information we need for our greater awareness, consciousness and growth are very complex and various. We are like the topmost twigs on the tree of ancient wisdom. Some of the dead wood is falling away and some branches are in full growth. One of them is the branch of Teilhard de Chardin, reaching out in many directions with green shoots of new truth, and older truth reorganized.

"*Good news!*
Liberty to captives!
Sight for the blind!
Freedom from oppression!"
-Luke 4:18

We find-
Christ's own manifesto.
For humanity, Love's leaven!
God's will is being done
On Earth as it is in Heaven.

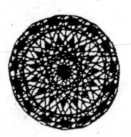

Love, the cohesive Spirit eternal, creates by uniting, and sustains identity in complexity. From beginning to end there is more and higher consciousness. 'The Spirit blows where it will' and should not be all tied up by fears and laws. As Teilhard says, 'Whatever is better will be.' The secret is to be always in Love, with the One above all, through all, and in all; to carefully protect and nourish that Love within every other Love, expressed according to the need of each, building the harmony and perfection of the Earth. The purpose is structure, to unite all things in their proper place and order, more like music than architecture, - an unending song.

We really do live in a make-believe world: First we believe and than we make it as we want it to be. By the year 2080 the Earth should be as obedient to the Spirit of Love as nature now is to instinct. We are always more aware in great union, and more united in great awareness. Teilhard calls it 'more being in greater union.'

The dichotomy between good en evil is simply that we cannot move in opposite directions at once. Either we move toward union (individual, social and cosmic) or we are moving toward disintegration. There is no place for any person or group outside the whole. Teilhard states unequivocally, 'The age of nations is past.' There is no point in saving an arm of a leg if the rest of the body dies.

Mutual dedication to the Mind above all, revealed in the universe, results in Love, bringing us to the realization that there is nothing, no time, no distance between us. The full power of history, physical and cultural is flowing through us. Time does not pass but accumulates; all our daily experiences become shared in a instant of transference, person to person. All our relationships are arranged in beauty; total love becomes structure, a structure of freedom in which every act comes from internal motivation and none from external coercion. That we may all be One.

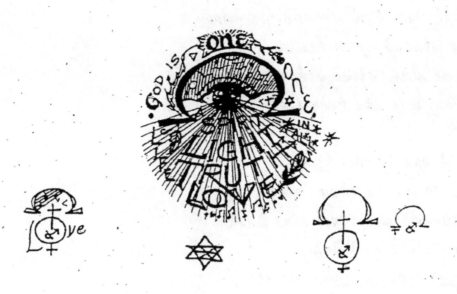

Our Father, inseminating Spirit and Light pervading all that is , Holy is your Nature. Your cohesive activity, LOVE, continues in Earth as in Heaven.

You give us, Daily, our food, and fulfill our needs as we fulfill the needs of others.

You lead us out of all kinds of evil, for yours is the goodness completing creation in the power of LOVE and the glory of Life Forever.   Amen.

The Resurrection

The body stiff as board
On the hard packed earth was laid
Darkened blood still poured
From the wound the spear had made
A cloth was tied around his jaw
Coins placed upon his eyes
A stone was rolled before the cave
And — there the body lies.

But Jesus is the <u>Light</u>
Not just an earthen lamp
And though the tomb was dark
And redolent and damp,
<u>Without</u> <u>moving</u> <u>sheet</u> or <u>stone</u>
It became as bright as day!
<u>The</u> <u>Light,</u> — (His Body) rose.
And somewhere far away
Officials felt a chill
Uncertain how they knew
The Christ was living still
And the prophecies were true.

RECONSIDER THE EVIDENCE: <u>THE SHROUD OF TURIN</u>. (IT HAS NEVER BEEN EXPLAINED.)

EASTER

Resurrection is expansion
As we die we rise
Face to face we see ourselves
And there our body lies!
Beginning our extended flight
We go swiftly, safely on
In beauty luminous and bright
Children of the Dawn.

Christ arose to "fill all things" 1.
The Universe awakes and sings!
There are scents and sounds and voices
Familiar from our past
Because we are "his body" 2.
We find that all things last!
"Christ brought immortality
(And Love) and life to light" 3.
In him are new dimensions
Open to our sight.

New light and truth continually
Illuminate the old
Accumulated evidence
Of centuries has told:
ETERNAL LIFE IS IN THE CHRIST 4.
AS CONSCIOUSNESS EXPANDS.
Love cherishes identity
And we are in Love's hands!
Never again to feel alone
"We shall know as we are known." 5.

1. Ephesians 4:10
2. 1 Corinth. 12:27
3. II Tim. 1:10
4. Ephesians 1:9 & 10
5. I Corinth. 13:12

Easter Carol

"Look now for glad and
golden hours
Come swiftly, on the wing.
Oh rest beside the weary
♪♪♫♪♪ road ♪♪♪♪
And hear the angels sing." — OLD CHRISTMAS CAROL

The eternal now is made
of all the past ~
Like our assimilated
childhood
Is all-at-once; at last.
Wholly one we meet ~
In meeting we are bound.
Changed and yet unchanging
In the timeless ONE we're found.

A THEOLOGICAL THEORY
A TERRIFYING RESPONSIBILITY

As the Spirit of God <u>enters</u> more and more into us and His creation (which began with the insemination of the world/Universe by his WORD)—information, consciousness, and <u>our control</u> of organization and order increases; (resulting at present in fragmentation and disorder.)

By the law of dissipative structures—(entropy) every increase in ordered complexity discharges disorder into the environment. God is our spiritual environment: "In Him we live and move and have our being." So God's direct, external control continuously decreases. <u>God loses more and more control to us,</u> who must then exert our responsibility for integrating and perfecting all things. God is becoming in us the Coming One. We are the son of God growing up into Him, completely, with the passage of all time. Jesus, as he said, is the Seed/Word planted in the Earth. In us, our "hope of glory."

According to recent studies of Entropy, chaos, (random dissipation) has the function of preceding new and higher levels of complexity. What we are now experiencing is the necessary disintegration of an old system so that a new one, higher and more complex, may be born. Truth is the arranging agent. Love is the cohesive power. <u>Sharing Truth Accomplishes union.</u> A sorting process!

God, "I Am", Being, is the eternal Source and <u>Existence</u> of this information WORD. His Truth, by Love, binds atoms and all else together. Our assimilation of Truth, and resulting interaction in Love, is the function of the conscious elements of the Becoming One. <u>Share TRUTH to know LOVE.</u> <u>God is uncreated,</u> infinite Potential. Life is the accumulation of complexity, infinite and eternal—including your identity and everything else! Rearranged, but bound forever—the music of the Universe.

THE LORD'S PRAYER

About forty years ago I began to study the Lord's Prayer. Throughout those forty years I have discovered that one never finishes the study! I think it has had a greater effect on my life than any other one thing. It continues to influence everything I think and do.

When Jesus' disciples asked him to teach them how to pray, he gave them a PATTERN for prayer. (See Luke 11:2 and Matt. 6:7). Or as Methodists might prefer, a METHOD of prayer. Jesus did not intend that people should mindlessly repeat the OUTLINE. He warned against piling up empty words. Our prayers should have the content of our minds and hearts.

Jesus did not tell his disciples, "It doesn't make and difference how you pray." He gave them DIRECTIONS for their praying, that would <u>help</u> them pray and live effectively.

One of the things an old friend of mine, Sam Reinke, pointed out to me is that the Greek aorist verb "to be" has no tense: it is past present and future. In English, the way I understand it, it should be translated "was, is, and to be". That is a little awkward. We can't do it all at once. So one way I pray the Lord's prayer is in the present tense.

Jesus said, "The Kingdom of God is at hand." It is not only in the future. We see God's Rule and Order all around us: in nature, in structure, in beauty, and in much that people accomplish in HUMAN life.

So let us consider the Lord's prayer in the <u>present tense.</u> How do we pray it now?

We begin by saying, "Our Father...." Jesus told us to call God "Father". I have a tendency to think that He knew what he was talking about! God has planted his Seed in the Earth. He did not create us with his hands! He <u>is</u> our Father. And we grow within the Earth (and eventually out of it.)

It is also good to remember other words to describe God, so that we have an idea for our minds to hold. God told Moses, "I AM THAT I AM". To me that means BEING, itself. John says that, "God is Love." Jesus, himself, said "Hear O Isreal, the Lord our God is ONE." He said. "God is Spirit." St.Paul said, "God is LIGHT." SPIRIT, BEING, LOVE, AND LIGHT (which is energy) are all very closely related. In Ephesians we find, "One God and Father of us all who is above all, and through all and in all." (Chapter 4:18.) This is a real and physical fact. It has become more and more real to me for the past forty years.

I can barely touch on a few phrases. The Lord's Prayer could be a lifetime study for all denominations. It is one thing in which all Christians find they are united.

After we say, "Our Father"/who is in Heaven" (above all, through all and in all) we say "Holy be thy name". In the present tense we would say, "Holy IS your name." "Your ORDER comes; Your will is being done on Earth as it is in the whole Universe." The process takes a long, long time. But as Teilhard de Chardin said, "WHATEVER IS BETTER WILL BE." He also said that the chaotic events we are experiencing are the pains of birth, not the pains of death. (See: Matt 24:7&8 and Mark 13:7&8)

Next we pray, "Give us this day our daily bread.": When I pray this part of the prayer, I say, "You give us this day our daily food; all the fruits of the Earth that we could never have planned or imagined."

The next part, "You forgive our debts as we forgive our debtors" means that God fulfills our needs as we fulfill the needs of others. (Besides much more.)

Then, "Lead us not into temptation" would be "You do not lead us into temptation but deliver us from all evil". When we really pay attention to all the good God has for us we are delivered from many kinds of evil. This mystery is best expressed in the book of John (3:8) "the WIND blows where it will, and you hear the sound of it, but you do not know where it comes from or where it is going; so it is with everyone who is born of the Spirit."

When we say, "For thine is the Kingdom", we are really confessing "For yours, O God, is the ORDER (and RULE of truth".)

..."and the Power".....The Power of Love, the force that draws and holds, all things together. By and in Love God creates everything that exists.

..."and the glory".....The glory of life forever. That is what Easter is all about: Life-in Love forever. And this life must begin here and now.

CHOOSE AND POST A FOLLOWING POSTER

<u>The Birth of God — theology</u>

We are different padrts of that body

— SEE I CORINTH. 12:14

Sown in the Earth.

— SEE MATT. 13:31

We shall grow up into him who is the head.

— SEE EPH. 4:15

— knowing as we are known.

— SEE 1 CORINTH. 13:12

For God did not send his son into the world to condemn the world, but that the World might be saved through him. (in us.)

— John 3:17

Belief in life after "death" is helped by understanding that the point(.) is contained in the line '(_____); the line is contained in the solid; the solid is contained in space/time;
EACH DIMENSION CONTAINS ALL THE PREVIOUS DIMENSIONS. The "Eternal NOW" is eternal: "Everything is saved."

-Teilhard

Orchestrate the Earth.

Listen —
Tune yourself
Follow the Maestro
Play.

△ ♡ <

12 verses —
the Essence of
Eternal
Love.

I tell you the truth:
whoever hears my words,
and believes in him who
sent me, has eternal

Life.

~John
5:24~

△ ♡ <

This, then, is what I
command you: ~

Love one
another.

~John 15:17

If you really knew what
"this scripture means,
I do not want animal
you sacrifices but Kindness,"
would not have con-
demned people who are
not guilty.

~ Matt. 12:7

△ ♡ <

Do not judge others and
God will not judge you;
do not condemn others, and
God will not condemn
you; forgive others and
God will forgive you.

~ Luke 6:37

Did not God, who made the outside, also make the inside? Give what is in your cups and plates to those in need and everything will be clean for you.

~Luke 11:40-41

△♡<

And when He comes He will prove to the people of the world that they are wrong about sin, and about what is right, and about God's judgement.

~John 16:8

The Lord our God is
One.
And you must love the
Lord your God with all
your heart, soul, mind,
and strength: Love your
neighbor as yourself.
~ Mark 12:30

△♡<

If anyone wants to
come with me,
he must forget him-
self, take up his cross
daily and follow, follow
me.

~ Luke 9:23

None of you can be my disciple ~ unless he gives everything he has.

~Luke 14:33

△♡<

Holy Father, keep them in thy nature, which thou hast given me, that they may be one ——, even as we are one.

~John 17:11

For he has made known to us in all wisdom and insight the mystery of his will, according to his purpose which he set forth in Christ as a plan for the fulness of time to unite all things in him — things in Heaven and things on Earth.

~Ephesians 1:9-10

△ ♡ <

Life in our —Time— requires faithful, progressive, inclusive, communicating LOVE. WHICH COMES FROM SHARING TRUTH AND BEAUTY.

New truth

with you always, to the close of the age.

FOR
GREETING
CARDS
CUT AND
PASTE

be ~
generous with ~
your body, mind,
soul and things.
"Truth is beauty
Beauty
Sings"

LOVE

LOVE

FAITHFUL - IDENTIFYING - CREATIVE INCLUSIVE - TIME GIVING -

Jesu. Islam

"The Lord is One". —MOSES — ABRAHAM
—MUHAMMAD
—JESUS, CHRIST

STUDY THE MASTERS —
SUBORDINATE ALL COMMENTARY

Being: I AM:

Above all; through all; in all.

God-All-ah-
PEACE

I was; I am; I will be

Jesus speaks of death as "sleep".[1]
It is a slumber long and deep.
In which we "reap what has been sown."
And when we "know as we are known."
We will travel among the oceans of stars.
And no more ravage the Earth with wars.
The wholeness of life we will understand:
We are unborn children in an unknown land.

Thomas took notes while Jesus taught.
And found the truth that he had sought:
     "The dead are not alive;
      And the living do not die."[2]
These words of Jesus tell us
Our deaths are like a sigh:
As here we wake, and nightly sleep,
We enter the familiar deep
Subconsciousness of death.
And dream. Life is one,
Without a seam.

By raising the son of the window of Nain,
And bringing Lazarus life again,
By healing the little girl, twelve years old,
He demonstrated what he told.
A description of life after death is elusive,
But by Love all time is structured, inclusive.
My past and present and future are me.
And I know, "Whatever is better will be."[3]

1. Concordance • 2. the Gospel According to Thomas
3. Teilhard de Chardin

170

IDENTIFIED

Christ in you, the hope of glory.
Col. 1:27

When I reflectively recall
Your touch, your eyes, your voice,
Everything about you---
I really have no choice
But to recognize and seek
The DIVINE PERSON-ality,
The banked and living FIRE,
That rare reality---
In you.   And so, alone,---
I look for you
In every passing face.
I dream and scheme and
                yearn-
In every time and place,
I see in you a height and
                depth
Beyond any I have known.
I see in you the LIGHT
I must try to make-
                my own.

The Law of Love

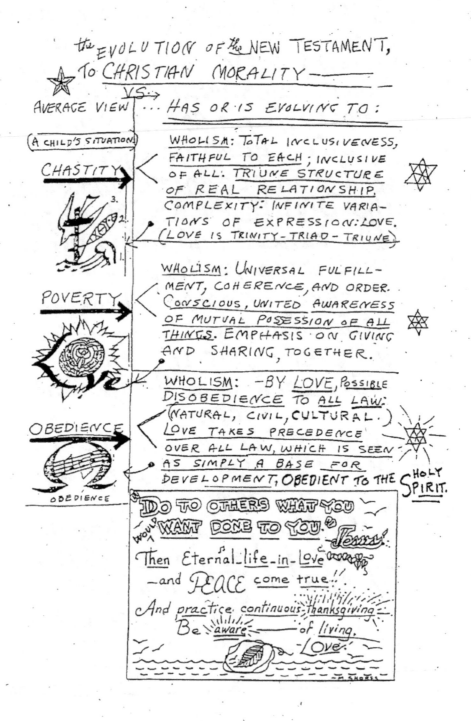

the EVOLUTION OF the NEW TESTAMENT,
★ TO CHRISTIAN MORALITY —

AVERAGE VIEW | VS. | ... HAS OR IS EVOLVING TO:

(A CHILD'S SITUATION)

CHASTITY

WHOLISM: TOTAL INCLUSIVENESS,
FAITHFUL TO EACH; INCLUSIVE
OF ALL. TRIUNE STRUCTURE
OF REAL RELATIONSHIP.
COMPLEXITY: INFINITE VARIA-
TIONS OF EXPRESSION: LOVE.
(LOVE IS TRINITY - TRIAD - TRIUNE)

POVERTY

WHOLISM: UNIVERSAL FULFILL-
MENT, COHERENCE, AND ORDER.
CONSCIOUS, UNITED AWARENESS
OF MUTUAL POSSESSION OF ALL
THINGS. EMPHASIS ON GIVING
AND SHARING, TOGETHER.

OBEDIENCE

OBEDIENCE

WHOLISM: — BY LOVE, POSSIBLE
DISOBEDIENCE TO ALL LAW:
(NATURAL, CIVIL, CULTURAL.)
LOVE TAKES PRECEDENCE
OVER ALL LAW, WHICH IS SEEN
AS SIMPLY A BASE FOR
DEVELOPMENT, OBEDIENT TO THE HOLY SPIRIT.

"DO TO OTHERS WHAT YOU
WOULD WANT DONE TO YOU." Jesus
Then Eternal life in Love
—and PEACE come true!!
And practice continuous thanksgiving —
Be aware of living.
—Love

Our sexuality is driven by the prehistoric need to perpetuate our kind, although humans are no longer limited to seasons, propagation or by gender. (Our sexuality can be expressed in bi-sexual or even "omni-sexual" ways.)

But we are called to a higher complexity and holiness which transcends the discontinuity of much genital-sexual expression, with-whole person love. Whole-Love controls the primitive sexual urge by creativity and bonding relationships. (We are made of our relationships, literally.)

The best Love is directed by the Spirit "above all, through all, and in all." We become Children of Light blending in the Holly One. When this life FORCE is arranged and ordered by the Spirit we find that Love is scheduled and inclusive, a mystery to reason.

The Golden Rule is always plural, and requires thought and consideration before our every act. "Do FOR OTHERS JUST WHAT YOU WOULD WANT THEM TO DO FOR YOU." The POWER to live in this way is in our genes—what we currently call "sex". The right use of this energy cannot be codified in laws but must be free to function according to the purpose of complete and complex consciousness for humanity, unforeseen, (or seen only in retrospect, one stage at a time.)

We are drawn by inner affinity to specific others, into the structure required for social survival and peace. Sexuality in human beings is a continually growing; changing incitement to evolution-of-consciousness; by complexification: The surpassing sublimation of inclusive Love; THE-FORCE IS WITH YOU.

NOTES:

173

by Maryann Shorey

The increasing <u>sexual energy</u>, everywhere out of control, must be channelled by <u>new satisfying rituals</u> into Spiritual <u>social structure</u>. Love is the problem; Love is the power; Love is the answer. The purpose of Love is structure. "Do unto others just what you want done to you" The Golden Rule is —<u>plural</u>=<u>Inclusive</u> Scheduled Love.

SUGGESTED BOOKS AND AUTHORS

1. ✿ EVERYTHING THAT WAS WRITTEN BY TEILHARD DE CHARDIN

2. Barrow, J. Tipler — The Anthropic Cosmological Principle

3. Boslough — Masters of Time

4. Briggs, J. Peal, D — Looking Glass Universe

5. Capra, F. — The Turning Point

6. Davies, P. — God and the New Physics

7. Dodson, E. — The Phenomenon of Man Revisited

8. Dyson, F. — Disturbing the Universe

9. Gorvan, John C. — Trance, Art and Creativity

10. Gebser — Ever Present Origin

11. Jantsch, E. — The Self-Organizing Universe

12. Kaiser, Chris — Creation and the History of Science

13. Lewin, Roger — Complexity - Life at the Edge of Chaos

14. Murchie, A. — The Seven Mysteries of Life

15. Moore, T. — Care of the Soul

16. Moore, T. — The New Jerusalem Bible

17. Peacock, Arthur — Theology for a Scientific Age

18. Russel, P. — The Global Brain

19. Sanford, John — The Kingdom Within

20. Templeton, Herrmann — The God Who Would Be Known

21. Young, L. — The Unfinished Universe

22. Zajonc — Catching the Light

23. Zonneveld, L., Muller R. — The Desire to be Human

24. Zonneveld, L — Humanity's Quest for Unity

25. A list of authors with complementary views:
    John Barrow
    Thomas Berry
    John B. Cobb
    Matthew Fox
    Thomas King (S.J.)
    John Polkinghorne
    Ilya Prigogine
    Karl Rahner
    Karl Schmitz-Moorman
    Allerd Stikker
    Brian Swimme
    Philip Hefner
    - et al (means - "and others")

"True Love differs from gold and clay,
To divide is not to take away."
—SHELLY

To Light One Candle From Another Increases The Fire.

SUGGESTIONS FOR USING THE TRIUNE LOVE WORKBOOK.

1. Small, invited Group of Young (not too young) Married Women. Show Video. Do Not Discuss. (Do not include verses on end of tape.)

2. Have black-board or easel available. Begin with page 74 - diagram - discuss.

3. Next read and discuss Jim's interview. p. 45. (Diagram as feasible.)

4. Return to beginning of book - read every page and discuss, in order. (Do not drag.)

5. Several sessions will be required to do the whole book. (You may terminate at any point.) If summary section is reached, use video and (this time) discuss.

6. Suggest personal use of this Book; and verses distilled from Teilhard during morning meditation times. (See John Roschen letter.)

7. Schedule next time and place.

AN AFTER WORD
(RUMINATIONS)

In the new book, <u>CONVERSATIONS WITH GOD</u>, by Neale Walsch, we find:

"Adding the third part of the Trinity produces this relationship: That which <u>gives</u> <u>rise</u> to/That which <u>is</u> <u>risen</u>/That which <u>is.</u>

This triune reality is God's signature. It is the divine pattern. The three-in one is everywhere found in the realms of the sublime. You cannot escape it in matters dealing with time and space, God and consciousness, or any of the subtle relationships. On the other hand, you will *not* find the Triune Truth in any of life's gross relationships. Hence, there is left-right, up-down, big-small, fast-slow, hot-cold, and the greatest dyad ever created: male-female. There are no *in-betweens* in these dyads. A thing is either *one thing or the other*, <u>or some greater or lesser version</u> gradation in relationship to one of these polarities. But when God/Spirit is included there is the "sublime," <u>TRIUNE LOVE.</u>

"The Triune Truth is recognized in life's subtle relationships by everyone dealing with such relationships. Some of your religionists have described the Triune Truth as Father, Son, and Holy Ghost. Some of your Psychiatrists use the terms superconscious, conscious and subconscious. Some of your spiritualist say mind, body, and spirit. Some of your scientists see energy, matter, ether. Some of your philosophers say a thing is not true for you until it is true in thought, word, and deed. When discussing time, you speak of three times only: past, present, future. Similarly, there are three moments in your perception—before, now, and after. In terms of spatial relationships, whether considering the points in the universe, or various points in your own room, you recognize here, there, and the space in between.

Within the realm of sublime relationships nothing which exists *has* an opposite. Time is a sublime realm, in which what you call past, present and future exist *inter-relationally.* That is they are not *opposite*, but rather parts of the same whole;"

An example of what God does with relationships is found in the result of god's action concerning David and Bathsheba, II Samuel 11.

Ancient Hebrew Sages report—...God had told David he would be unable to withstand the temptation of Bat Sheva, and so David capitulated, though he would have been able to resist if left to his own devices (Feuer, 654). So, in verse 4, David reminds God of his obedience when he says, "so that Your words would be justified / So that You will be right in Your verdict." David now merits God's forgiveness because he did as God expected. (*Psalm 51) So in Matthew's genealogy, Chapters one, we find Bathsheba (Bat Seva) was necessary for the earthly birth of the man, Jesus. See also footnote in New Jerusalem Bible, to Matthew 2:5* which states that some ancient authorities use the phrase "Joseph fathered Jesus." (Considered an error by the translators). *see Luke 1:33 & 35.

Maybe Jesus was sent from a distant Star, half Alien to the Earth? See John 3:13-17 and 3:31, also John 6: 33, 38, 51, 58, 62. etc. Or maybe a third element was added to the two earthly progenitors? What we call angels, visions, some dreams, etc. may be the intrusion of another dimension, part of our Universe as yet unaccepted. The Universe, one functioning whole, is greater and stranger than we like to admit. We need to keep an open mind but not so open our brains fall out! After all brain/consciousness is the evident purpose of the complexity of life.

Name	Area Code	Telephone Number

CPSIA information can be obtained
at www.ICGtesting.com
Printed in the USA
LVHW101258230119
604953LV00003B/91/P